D1104005

psychological disorders related to

DESIGNER DRUGS

THE ENCYCLOPEDIA OF PSYCHOLOGICAL DISORDERS

- **Anorexia Nervosa:**
  Starving for Attention

- **Child Abuse and Neglect:**
  Examining the Psychological Components

- **Conduct Unbecoming:**
  Hyperactivity, Attention Deficit, and Disruptive Behavior Disorders

- **Cutting the Pain Away:**
  Understanding Self-Mutilation

- **Drowning Our Sorrows:**
  Psychological Effects of Alcohol Abuse

- **Life Out of Focus:**
  Alzheimer's Disease and Related Disorders

- **The Mental Effects of Heroin**

- **Psychological Disorders Related to Designer Drugs**

- **Psychological Effects of Cocaine and Crack Addiction**

- **Schizophrenia:**
  Losing Touch with Reality

- **Sibling Rivalry:**
  Relational Disorders Involving Brothers and Sisters

- **Smoke Screen:**
  Psychological Disorders Related to Nicotine Use

- **Through a Glass Darkly:**
  The Psychological Effects of Marijuana and Hashish

- **The Tortured Mind:**
  The Many Faces of Manic Depression

- **When Families Fail:**
  Psychological Disorders Caused by Parent-Child Relational Problems

- **A World Upside Down and Backwards:**
  Reading and Learning Disorders

THE ENCYCLOPEDIA OF PSYCHOLOGICAL DISORDERS

Senior Consulting Editor Carol C. Nadelson, M.D.
Consulting Editor Claire E. Reinburg

psychological disorders related to

DESIGNER DRUGS

Elizabeth Russell Connelly

CHELSEA HOUSE PUBLISHERS
Philadelphia

The ENCYCLOPEDIA OF PSYCHOLOGICAL DISORDERS provides up-to-date information on the history of, causes and effects of, and treatment and therapies for problems affecting the human mind. The titles in this series are not intended to take the place of the professional advice of a psychiatrist or mental health care professional.

Chelsea House Publishers
Editor in Chief: Stephen Reginald
Managing Editor: James D. Gallagher
Production Manager: Pamela Loos
Art Director: Sara Davis
Director of Photography: Judy L. Hasday
Senior Production Editor: LeeAnne Gelletly

Staff for PSYCHOLOGICAL DISORDERS RELATED TO DESIGNER DRUGS
Picture Researcher: Sandy Jones
Associate Art Director: Takeshi Takahashi
Designer: 21st Century Publishing and Communications, Inc.
Cover Designer: Brian Wible

The Chelsea House World Wide Web site address is http://www.chelsea house.com

First Printing

1 3 5 7 9 8 6 4 2

Library of Congress Cataloging-in-Publication Data

Connelly, Elizabeth Russell.
Psychological disorders related to designer drugs / by Elizabeth Russell Connelly.
  p. cm. — (Encyclopedia of psychological disorders)
Includes bibliographical references and index.
Summary: Examines the history, nature, effects, and dangers of such designer drugs as Ecstasy, PCP, fentanyl, and meperidine.
ISBN 0-7910-4957-4 (hardcover)
1. Designer drugs—United States Juvenile literature. 2.Designer drugs—United States—Psychological aspects Juvenile lirerarture. 3. Drug abuse—United States Juvenile literature. 4. Teenagers—Drug use—United States Juvenile literature. [1. Designer drugs. 2. Drugs. 3. Drug abuse.] I. Title. II. Series
HV5825.C636   1999   99-13437
362.29'9—dc21   CIP
                                                                      AC

CONTENTS

PSYCHOLOGICAL DISORDERS AND THEIR EFFECT

CAROL C. NADELSON, M.D.
PRESIDENT AND CHIEF EXECUTIVE OFFICER,
The American Psychiatric Press

There are a wide range of problems that are considered psychological disorders, including mental and emotional disorders, problems related to alcohol and drug abuse, and some diseases that cause both emotional and physical symptoms. Psychological disorders often begin in early childhood, but during adolescence we see a sharp increase in the number of people affected by these disorders. It has been estimated that about 20 percent of the U.S. population will have some form of mental disorder sometime during their lifetime. Some psychological disorders appear following severe stress or trauma. Others appear to occur more often in some families and may have a genetic or inherited component. Still other disorders do not seem to be connected to any cause we can yet identify. There has been a great deal of attention paid to learning about the causes and treatments of these disorders, and exciting new research has taught us a great deal in the past few decades.

The fact that many new and successful treatments are available makes it especially important that we reject old prejudices and outmoded ideas that consider mental disorders to be untreatable. If psychological problems are identified early, it is possible to prevent serious consequences. We should not keep these problems hidden or feel shame that we or a member of our family has a mental disorder. Some people believe that something they said or did caused a mental disorder. Some people think that these disorders are "only in your head" so that you could "snap out of it" if you made the effort. This type of thinking implies that a treatment is a matter of willpower or motivation. It is a terrible burden for someone who is suffering to be blamed for his or her misery, and often people with psychological disorders are not treated compassionately. We hope that the information in this book will teach you about various mental illnesses.

The problems covered in the volumes of the ENCYCLOPEDIA OF PSYCHOLOGICAL DISORDERS were selected because they are of particular importance to young adults, because they affect them directly, or because they affect family and friends. There are individual volumes on reading disorders, attention deficit and disruptive behavior disorders, and dementia—all of these are related to our abilities to learn and integrate information from the world around us. There are books on drug abuse that provide useful information about the effects of these drugs and treatments that are available for those individuals who have drug problems. Some of the books concentrate on one of the most common mental disorders, depression. Others deal with eating disorders, which are dangerous illnesses that affect a large number of young adults, especially women.

Most of the public attention paid to these disorders arises from a particular incident involving a celebrity that awakens us to our own vulnerability to psychological problems. These incidents of celebrities or public figures revealing their own psychological problems can also enable us to think about what we can do to prevent and treat these types of problems.

Teenagers are the most likely to use "designer" drugs such as Ecstasy, GHB, or crystal methamphetamine; these laboratory-created alternatives to traditional drugs, such as marijuana, cocaine, or heroin are usually as inexpensive and readily available as they are dangerous.

DESIGNER DRUGS: AN OVERVIEW

"**J**ust say no." Since the mid-1980s, that's what most teenagers have heard when they asked adults about drugs. Unfortunately, this and other responses to the problem of young adults using drugs in the United States have not been enough. Teens clearly want something substantial and credible to convince them that drugs are a waste of time. They hear their friends and classmates talking about how much fun they've had with drugs. More than likely, these friends don't remember much about themselves on drugs, and can't tell if they acted irrationally or stupidly; but they often believe that they are more hip and exciting when they're high. Young adults—whether they are in middle school, junior high, or high school—need more than sensible explanations of the actual risks involved in taking drugs; they need support and treatment if they carry drug use too far. The purpose of this book is to provide teens with the facts about designer drugs and their effect on the human brain and body.

Many teens experiment with drugs as part of the usual course of growing up. In a nationwide study conducted in 1998 by the National Institute on Drug Abuse (NIDA), 45 percent of high school seniors report having used illicit drugs at least once, and 30 percent acknowledge having used them before high school. Those who use drugs regularly during their teenage years can develop problems with their psychological, emotional, and social development.

An example is Dan, who comes from a comfortable, middle-class urban family. He had always done very well in school and was fairly ambitious, with plans to go on to college. During his freshman year of high school, he started drinking beer and smoking pot (marijuana) at parties. By the end of the school year, he had added LSD to the mix and was frequently getting high during the day. Later in Dan's sophomore year, a friend offered him some Ecstasy, which became his main—but by no means only—drug of choice for several years.

In Dan's mind, his drug use was only recreational, something he could quit anytime he wanted, but he just didn't want to. He applied to and was accepted at a few colleges, with some offering him scholarships. But he blew off the interviews. A friend's mother got him a job as a doorman; he quit two days later. He stole money from friends and family members, then struck out on his own. After a few years of stealing or doing odd jobs for drug money, and occasionally living on the streets, Dan fell into a long, deep depression. Finally, after a counselor found him and eventually got through to him, Dan began to remember some of his old ambitions. At the age of 22 and after about one year in treatment, he reapplied to college. Dan still undergoes therapy, but is also now studying to be a kindergarten teacher.

Dan's story points to the consequences of drug abuse. Over and over, in his selfish quest for the next high, he hurt family and friends. He resorted to crime to support his habit, and he wasted years of his life in a downward spiral. In one way, Dan is much more fortunate than many who become addicted to drugs: he's getting a second chance. Too many become pathetic slaves to their habits, or wind up dying from a drug overdose.

One problem with designer drugs is the danger of uncertainty. Each batch "cooked up" by amateur chemists in illegal, home-based labs contains many impurities and toxins. As a result, a drug's effect on its user may change each time he or she takes the substance. Sometimes there are serious, even lethal, consequences. Users may unknowingly take a dose that is too strong, causing a fatal overdose. The toxins in a drug may cause permanent brain damage or death. And users who combine drugs, believing they'll have a more intense high, may discover too late that they have mixed themselves a deadly cocktail.

This volume of the ENCYCLOPEDIA OF PSYCHOLOGICAL DISORDERS examines the most popular new "designer" drugs: GHB, Ecstasy, and derivatives of methamphetamine, phencyclidine (PCP), fentanyl, and meperidine (MPPP). Chapter 1 introduces readers to the world of designer drugs. Chapter 2 offers some perspective by outlining the history of drugs in general, as well as the origins of each designer drug. Chapter 3 explores what prompts adolescents to use drugs in the first place, and chapter 4 delves deeper into the actual effects users might experience with each type of designer drug. Chapter 5 analyzes the impact of designer drugs on society as a whole, and chapter 6 highlights the most commonly used methods for treating problems associated with drug use today.

A close-up photograph of large and small tablets of Ecstasy. The small pills are stamped with doves; the amateur chemists who create the tablets often mark them in a distinctive way.

1

WHAT ARE DESIGNER DRUGS?

Ecstasy, methamphetamine, "angel dust," "scoop"—these are names or nicknames for some of the more popular "designer drugs" used by teens today. These substances were created synthetically to mimic the effects of other medications or of drugs that come from natural sources, such as marijuana or cocaine. They're called designer drugs because they're specially designed and constantly modified by the people who make them. These designer drugs are meant to produce the same effects as the drugs they mimic, but in many cases they are much stronger and much more addictive. They're also illegal.

In general, illicit drugs become available in the United States through a variety of sources. For example, drugs like heroin and cocaine are usually smuggled into the United States from foreign countries such as Mexico or Thailand; other drugs, such as marijuana, may be grown domestically. There are other drugs that are made by legitimate pharmaceutical companies but illegally diverted to the street market. But the designer drugs have yet another source: they are created in illegal laboratories by unlicensed and, usually, untrained amateurs, then distributed in the local area around that lab.

These clandestine laboratories began springing up in the 1960s and 1970s in response to a government clampdown on illegal drugs like heroin, cocaine, and marijuana; the increased vigilance made it more difficult for dealers and users to acquire these drugs. Illegal labs have been found in remote mountain cabins and rural farms, as well as in single and multifamily homes in city and suburban neighborhoods. These operations can be moved fairly quickly to new locations, in order to avoid detection by police or federal Drug Enforcement Administration (DEA) agents.

Just what it takes to set up a lab depends largely on the drug being synthesized. The production of some substances—crystal methamphetamine, PCP, or Ecstasy, for example—requires little sophisticated equipment or knowledge of chemistry. The people who make these drugs may have minimal or no training in chemistry, and often follow simple formulas, called recipes. Other drugs, such as fentanyl and its derivatives, require much higher levels of chemical expertise and more specialized equipment. Chemistry students or pharmaceutical professionals have the understanding to make these drugs. But in all cases, the laboratories are unsupervised and, unlike a professional drug manufacturing plant, there is no quality control to ensure the safety of the drug's user. One of the major risks involved in taking designer drugs is that the people who make them may be careless, or are more concerned with making money than with the user's safety.

Each of the drugs classified as a designer drug goes by many other street names, depending on when and where it is made and who makes it. Because each drug is based on a particular chemical compound, the following information is organized according to the drug's chemical name and lists various street names.

METHAMPHETAMINE

Methamphetamine is a stimulant—a drug that affects the brain, respiratory, circulatory, and central nervous systems by providing a temporary increase in their functional activity. It is one of a group of stimulants called amphetamines, but it produces stronger reactions in users than most other amphetamines. Like other amphetamines, methamphetamine causes increased brain activity, decreased appetite, and a general sense of well-being that can last for six to eight hours.

The white, odorless, and bitter-tasting crystalline powder is extremely addictive and easily dissolved in water or alcohol. Street names for methamphetamine include "Ice," "chalk," "crank," "cristy," "crystal meth," "glass," "go-fast," "LA," "meth," "quartz," "speed," and "zip." The slang term for someone who uses methamphetamine is that the person is "into powders."

In the 1960s, methamphetamine hydrochloride, nicknamed "speed," was the most popular form of the drug. Today the most common substance is a more powerful crystalline methamphetamine solution known on the street as "crystal meth" or "Ice" because of the drug's appearance in clear crystal chunks. Referred to as the "cocaine of the '90s," due both to its popularity and its cocaine-like effects, crystal meth is less expensive than cocaine, making it much more attractive to teens.

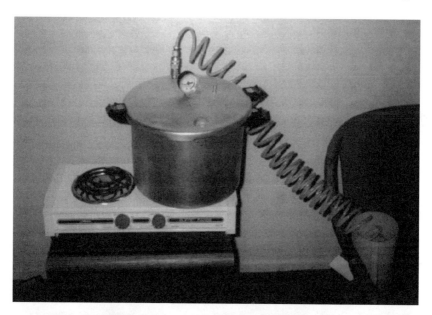

The top photo shows a crude device used to prepare methamphetamine. The illegal lab was found in an Oklahoma home in 1997 by federal Drug Enforcement Administration agents. Both the equipment and the ingredients required to "cook" methamphetamine can be acquired easily; this is one of the reasons for the drug's low cost and consequent popularity. In the bottom photo, taken in 1998, anti-drug agents carry bottles containing methamphetamine from a Philadelphia garage where the drug was manufactured.

Doctor Michael Abrams, a specialist from a medical center in Des Moines, Iowa, explains the effects of methamphetamine on the brain at a field hearing of the U.S. Senate Caucus on International Narcotics Control. Drugs like Ice, Ecstasy, PCP, and types of synthetic heroin like fentanyl or meperidine can have a detrimental long-term effect on a user's brain.

Crystal meth is typically smoked in a glass pipe like crack cocaine; the smoke is odorless, leaves a residue that can be resmoked, and produces effects that may continue for 12 hours or more. The drug can also be inhaled through the nose (snorted) or injected directly into the bloodstream with a hypodermic syringe. According to the White House Office of Drug Control Policy, the way that methamphetamine is commonly taken varies according to the region of the country and the age group of the user. In San Francisco, for example, injection is the preferred route; in Honolulu, it's smoking. In Phoenix, younger users tend to opt for pills, while older users prefer to snort the powder.

Smoking and injecting are the fastest ways to deliver the drug to the brain. By either method, users get very high very rapidly. After the initial "rush" of sensation, many users become highly agitated; the behavior of some may escalate to violence. Stimulants like methamphetamine are often used in a "binge and crash" pattern. Because the pleasurable effects of methamphetamine fade fairly quickly, before the drug concentration in the blood falls significantly, users try to maintain the high by repeatedly using it (binging) until their body is exhausted (crashing).

Under the federal Controlled Substances Act (CSA), methamphetamine is categorized as a Schedule II stimulant, which means it has a high potential for abuse and is available for medical purposes only through a nonrefillable prescription. The few accepted medical reasons for its use include treatment of narcolepsy (a sleep disorder characterized by sudden periods of deep sleep), attention-deficit hyperactivity disorder, and, for short-term use, obesity. But these medical uses are limited and carefully regulated.

HOW POPULAR IS METHAMPHETAMINE?

According to the 1996 *Monitoring the Future* study issued by the National Institute on Drug Abuse (NIDA), 4.4 percent of high school seniors admitted to using crystal methamphetamine at least once. This marked a significant increase over the 2.7 percent who admitted use in 1990. Of the same group, nearly 3 percent had used crystal methamphetamine in the year prior to the survey, doubling the number (1.3 percent) of the 1990 study. According to the White House Office of National Drug Control Policy's quarterly report *Pulsecheck* (Summer 1997), methamphetamine is second only to crack cocaine in popularity.

Data from a 1996 Drug Abuse Warning Network (DAWN) survey, which collected information on drug-related episodes from hospital emergency wards in 21 cities, showed that although meth-related episodes decreased between 1994 and 1996, there was a significant increase in these cases between the first and second halves of 1996 (from 4,000 to 6,800). NIDA's Community Epidemiology Work Group (CEWG), a network of researchers that provides information about drug use in major cities, reported in its June 1997 publication that methamphetamine abuse continues to be a problem in Hawaii, as well as in major cities such as San Francisco, Denver, and Los Angeles. Increased methamphetamine availability and production are being reported in diverse areas of the country, particularly rural areas, prompting concern about more widespread use.

MDMA (ECSTASY)

The chemical name for the drug commonly known as Ecstasy is 3,4-methylenedioxy-methamphetamine, or MDMA, a derivation of methamphetamine and amphetamine. MDMA is a synthetic drug that acts simultaneously as a stimulant and a hallucinogen, which means that it not only speeds up the body's functions but also can cause the user to see or hear things that aren't really there. These hallucination-causing drugs are also known as psychedelics. Ecstasy is most often found in tablet, capsule, or powder form and is usually swallowed, although it can be snorted or injected. It is sometimes packaged in capsules or generic tablets to imitate prescription drugs. The price of Ecstasy usually ranges from $20 to $40 per dose. Other nicknames for this drug include "X," "E," "X-TC," "Adam," "clarity," "essence," "lover's speed," and "Stacy."

Many users take Ecstasy because it makes them feel happy and care-free, excited, and at ease with themselves and others. Others take it because it distorts their senses, or because it provides an energy boost that helps them to stay awake through popular all-night dance parties known as "raves." Users who take Ecstasy at raves risk exhaustion and dehydration from a combination of the drug and nonstop dancing, and several have died from heat stroke. Also, because Ecstasy is often combined with other drugs—alcohol, LSD, heroin, fentanyl, or strong anesthetics—it can cause unpredictable reactions.

HOW POPULAR IS ECSTASY?

Ecstasy is the most common designer drug. While its use by college students has increased in recent years, MDMA is also being used by America's eighth, tenth, and twelfth graders. In the 1996 *Monitoring the Future* study, nearly 5 percent of tenth and twelfth graders, and about 2 percent of eighth graders, said they had used MDMA in the past year. Ecstasy is commonly available in at least 21 states and Canada, according to the Drug Enforcement Administration.

PHENCYCLIDINE (PCP)

Although PCP—often called by its most common nickname, "angel dust"—is illegal, it is easily manufactured in unsophisticated laboratories

WHERE DESIGNER DRUGS ARE USED

Designer drugs are widely used at "raves"–huge, all-night parties that are usually held in abandoned warehouses, parks, railroad yards, or night-clubs. Sometimes several thousand people–mostly teenagers and college students–will attend a rave to socialize and to dance to high-volume, computer-generated "techno" music. Though some legitimate nightclubs offer special "rave nights," most raves are illegal and can be very unsafe. In fact, there have been deaths and many injuries caused by floors caving in under the weight of too many dancers. This is in addition to deaths caused directly by the drugs taken at these parties.

Many rave attendees take drugs such as crystal meth or Ecstasy to provide energy during the frenetic, all-night dancing and to accentuate the driving beat of the music.

Although raves are the most popular place to take drugs, some people prefer to try them with friends at someone's house or at smaller parties. A quiet location may make them feel safer, but the effects of the drugs don't change.

from simple materials. PCP was first introduced as a street drug in the late 1960s and quickly gained a reputation as a drug that could cause bad reactions. In its pure form, PCP is a white crystalline powder that dissolves easily in water or alcohol. However, most PCP on the street contains a number of contaminants as a result of makeshift manufacturing, causing the color to range from tan to brown and the consistency from powder to a gummy mass.

The intensity and duration of the effects of PCP are wildly unpredictable. Because the potency of PCP varies widely, doses of the drug can produce different effects; some may be similar to those caused by stimulants or hallucinogens, while others act as painkillers. Not all people react the same way to the drug every time they take it, even when they take the same amount of the drug from the same batch.

PCP can be swallowed as a liquid, tablet, or capsule; snorted as a powder; or injected. The high generally lasts two to four hours, although the effects can continue as long as a day, and users may experience aftereffects that last for a few days. It also can be smoked in "joints" mixed with a leafy material, such as oregano, tobacco, or marijuana.

Street names for PCP include "cadillac," "crystal," "DOA," "dummy mist," "dust," "elephant tranquilizer" or "horse tranquilizer," "embalming fluid," and "zombie dust." When PCP is mixed with marijuana, the resulting drug is often called "crystal supergrass" or "killer joints." Blunts (joints of marijuana containing rocks of crack cocaine) that are dipped in PCP go by street names such as "happy sticks," "wicky sticks," "illies," "love boat," or "tical." New street names for PCP pop up so regularly that it has been suggested that any new drug with a bizarre name that is smoked or snorted can be assumed to involve PCP until proven otherwise.

HOW POPULAR IS PCP?

NIDA's 1996 *Monitoring the Future* study shows that after declining steadily from 1979 to 1993 the use of PCP among high school seniors has started to climb again, from 1.8 percent in 1995 to 2.6 percent in 1996. According to the 1996 National Household Survey on Drug Abuse, 3.2 percent of the population aged 12 and older have used PCP at least once.

Because the drug's reputation for bad reactions is well deserved, many people, after using the drug once, will not knowingly use it again. Yet others use it regularly, in many cases claiming that it gives them feelings of strength, power, and invulnerability. PCP can also numb the mind, causing anger and rage. "Bad trips" (negative experiences from a drug) can cause users to hallucinate, black out, and suffer muscle stiffness and tremors.

In many cases, because PCP is often mixed with or identified incorrectly as other drugs, the users do not realize they are ingesting it until it is too late. The following recollection from the 1986 book *Designer Drugs* indicates how PCP affected one unsuspecting user:

> I was out drinking beer. . . . This guy shows me a vial with a bunch of tabs he says are THC [tetrahydrocannabinol, the active ingredient in marijuana]. He warned me it was 100 percent pure and if I take one I should watch out for diarrhea. . . . I took one with my beer. . . . And when I started out of the bathroom 20 minutes later, I swear I was wearing twenty-foot stilts and was afraid of smashing my head through the ceiling. Then, as I'm trying to figure out how

Young adults entering a Florida dance club located in an old warehouse. Drugs like Ecstasy and GHB gained popularity at all-night dances that featured pounding "techno" music. The drugs are used at these events, called "raves," to boost energy and enhance sensation.

far away my legs are, I start hallucinating in all the primary colors. My arms and legs had gone numb and didn't exist and I was floating down the sidewalk—floating about fifty feet in the air. Later on, somebody told me it was PCP, not THC.

As this man found out, many people who use PCP may do it unknowingly. Often, drug dealers falsely present it as some other drug, such as mescaline, THC, or peyote. And because PCP is also often added to marijuana, LSD, and methamphetamine, unsuspecting users

HERBAL ECSTASY

The synthetic drug Ecstasy should not be confused with herbal ecstasy, a combination of herbs that is legal, inexpensive, and marketed as providing a "natural high." Herbal ecstasy can be purchased over the counter in drug stores, music stores, and shops around the country. The packaging on these products promises increased energy, heightened sexual sensitivity, and "cosmic consciousness." Users report feeling relaxed, tingly, and energetic.

Herbal ecstasy is composed of the Chinese herb *ma huang* (ephedrine) or a synthetic variation called pseudoephedrine, along with the herb koala nut, which provides caffeine. These ingredients are stimulants that together closely simulate the effects of Ecstasy. Sold in tablet form, herbal ecstasy is sometimes nicknamed "cloud 9," "herbal bliss," or "rave energy."

Although herbal ecstasy is not currently classified as a controlled substance, problems have arisen because there is no control over its manufacture and the amount of ephedrine and caffeine in the pills may vary widely. Over 800 reports of adverse reactions such as high blood pressure, seizures, heart attacks, strokes, and death have led the Food and Drug Administration (FDA) to consider placing restrictions on the drug.

who are anticipating the effects of these drugs may suddenly experience the stronger and unpredictable effects of PCP—or a deadly side effect resulting from the combination.

FENTANYL

Fentanyl was developed by a pharmaceutical company for use as a painkiller during surgical procedures. It was originally meant as a nonaddictive synthetic replacement for heroin, which itself had originally been developed at the turn of the century to replace morphine. However, each of these painkillers turned out to be more addictive than the one it replaced, and all eventually found their way into the illegal drug market.

In the United States, more than a dozen different designer drugs have been produced from fentanyl for recreational use. The most commonly

A packet of herbal ecstasy, along with pamphlets about its use. This combination of herbs is legal, inexpensive, and, users claim, mimics the effects of ecstasy. However, although not a restricted substance, herbal ecstasy is not without side effects.

known type is fentanyl alpha-methylfentanyl, which usually appears as a white powder and is nicknamed "China White." Other street names include "goodfella," "synthetic heroin," and "Tango and Cash."

Fentanyl is an opioid—a drug that is synthetically produced to relieve pain just as the natural derivatives of the opium poppy *papaver somniferum* do. These natural derivatives, called opiates, include opium, morphine, and heroin. Like the opiates and other opioids, fentanyl can produce an intense feeling of pleasure followed by a sense of well-being and a calm drowsiness. But the high from fentanyl-based drugs is short-lived—about 30 minutes to two hours—which means that users must take it more often to maintain their buzz. And like heroin and morphine, fentanyl is highly addictive. The more a person uses the drug, the more likely it is that the user will become physically and psychologically dependent on the drug.

One of the dangers of opioids lies in their unpredictable potency. For example, fentanyl can be up to 1,000 times more powerful than heroin, depending on how it's made. And because it's made in illegal labs without safety controls, no one can know how potent a dose is until it's too late. This means that fentanyl-based drugs have a high potential for overdose and death. According to the White House Office of National Drug Control Policy, the lethal effects of China White can be so sudden that many victims who injected the drug have been found dead with the needles still in their arms.

Most users smoke cigarettes laced with fentanyl or snort the powder. Although some inject it under their skin (skin-popping) or directly into a vein (mainlining), the fear of being exposed to HIV through shared needles has turned many away from these methods. Unfortunately, as users become addicted, the craving for a more powerful rush may lead addicts to try these dangerous procedures to get high.

There is not much information on street use of fentanyl; most statistics focus only on the many deaths that fentanyl has caused. Its use typically increases when heroin is scarce.

MEPERIDINE (MPPP)

Meperidine, known by the pharmaceutical trade name of Demerol, is considered to be a Schedule II narcotic under the Controlled Substances Act (CSA). Schedule II substances have a high potential for abuse as well as some recognized medical use. Demerol has a legitimate medical use as a potent pain reliever, mainly during childbirth and surgery. Because of its feel-good effects, however, meperidine is often abused as a recreational drug.

Though several meperidine-based designer drugs have been produced for illegal use, two appear to be more common on the streets: MPPP (1-methyl-4-phenyl-4-propionoxypiperidine) and PEPAP (1-[2-phenylethyl]-4-acetyloxypiperdine). When it is injected, MPPP produces a euphoria similar to that produced by heroin. Typically a white powder, MPPP has also been sold as an amber-colored powder with large granular crystals, which are dissolved in water and injected. Meperidine can also be swallowed as tablets or syrups.

The manufacture of meperidine requires sophisticated lab equipment and a knowledgeable chemist. As mentioned earlier, when drugs are created illegally there is always a risk that a careless or inexperienced chemist will inadvertently create poisonous by-products. With

A law-enforcement official with drugs, guns, and money seized in a $3 million drug bust. While making and selling drugs can be a dangerous business, using substances like China White or PCP can be even more dangerous.

meperidine, an impurity called MPTP (1-methyl-4-phenyl-1,2,3,6,-tetrahydro-pyridine) can be formed if sloppy "cooks" take shortcuts in the heating process. MPTP is a toxic compound that zeroes in on a section of the brain that controls movement and can cause irreversible brain damage there. The physical effects resemble severe symptoms of Parkinson's disease, a neurological condition; these include uncontrollable shaking of limbs, drooling, extreme muscle stiffness, and difficulty in moving and speaking.

Although it appears that illegal use of meperidine has declined in recent years—possibly as a result of increased availability and purity of heroin—it could re-emerge in response to the decreasing availability of other drugs. Historically the illegal use of meperidine over the past decade has increased during periods when heroin was scarce. Street names for the drug include "new heroin," "synthetic Demerol," and "synthetic heroin."

GAMMA-HYDROXYBUTYRIC ACID (GHB)

GHB is another drug that was originally developed as a painkiller but later withdrawn from common medical use due to its unwanted side effects. GHB is considered a depressant; it slows down body functions by depressing the central nervous system. In the United States, GHB was at one time used as an experimental treatment of narcolepsy. In Europe, GHB has been used as a painkiller and, in experiments, to treat the symptoms of alcohol withdrawal. The drug is marketed in England as an anti-aging medicine that allegedly increases the libido, decreases body fat, aids alcohol withdrawal, and induces sleep. But GHB's effectiveness in these areas is questionable.

There is no evidence yet that the drug is physically addictive or that it produces long-term negative effects. Currently, the greatest concern is the user's immediate reaction to varying doses of GHB. Those who use the drug maintain that small doses make them feel less inhibited and increase their sexual desire, causing a "drunk" feeling similar to the effects of alcohol (another depressant). However, higher doses can produce dangerous reactions, causing nausea, seizures, and in some cases, coma. GHB has also gained some notoriety as a "date-rape drug," since the odorless and nearly tasteless powder can be slipped undetected into someone's drink, causing the person to pass out. This leaves the victim open to, and defenseless against, sexual assault.

In recent years, GHB has become a popular drug in dance clubs and among partygoers. The compound can be taken orally, either in capsule form or as a grainy, whitish powder. Some users dissolve the powder in water or alcohol and drink it, while others snort or smoke the drug. It is most frequently sold as a slightly salty, clear liquid in small bottles that are bought by the capful or by the teaspoon. Nicknames for GHB include "cherry meth," "fantasy," "gamma 10," "Georgia home boy," "grievous bodily harm," "G-riffick," "liquid ecstasy," "scoop," and "zonked."

Once ingested, GHB begins to take effect within 5 to 20 minutes, the high lasts about one-and-a-half to three hours. Some users take GHB as a sedative to "come down" from the effects of stimulants like ephedrine, Ecstasy, speed, or cocaine. An especially dangerous habit is mixing GHB with alcohol or another depressant because the combination can slow the body's functions too quickly, causing coma or death.

HOW POPULAR IS GHB?

GHB can be made in basement chemistry labs relatively easily, and it can be synthesized from lye and industrial solvents that are commonly available. As a result, the drug is both easily available and inexpensive (from $3 to $10 per dose), and it is gaining popularity as an alternative to Ecstasy or speed.

Although use of GHB is still rare compared to that of other designer drugs, data from the Drug Abuse Warning Network (DAWN) strongly suggest that there has been an increase in its abuse since 1992. Most of the problem cases tracked by DAWN have taken place in the western United States. A 1997 report by the Substance Abuse and Mental Health Services Administration indicated that between 1992 and 1996, the number of GHB-related emergency-room visits went from 20 to 79 in Dallas, 0 to 103 in Los Angeles, 0 to 83 in San Francisco, 0 to 33 in Atlanta, 0 to 32 in San Diego, and 0 to 29 in Chicago. Two-thirds of the victims were white males between the ages of 18 and 25, while the other cases involved boys and girls under 18. Most had taken GHB with alcohol; several had also mixed it with cocaine, marijuana, or Ecstasy.

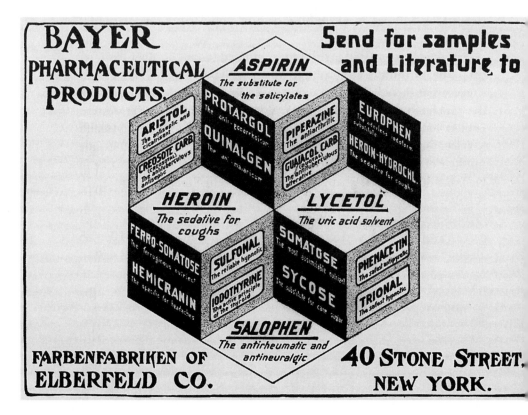

Drugs such as marijuana, alcohol, and opium have been used by humans for thousands of years; more recently, other drugs have been created by scientists. For example, in 1898 the Bayer pharmaceutical company developed heroin as a nonaddictive painkiller. This Bayer advertisement shows how heroin was initially sold as a pain reliever and cough medicine—until its addictive properties were discovered. The designer drugs that have become popular in the last three decades mimic the effects of drugs such as heroin.

2

THE HISTORY OF DESIGNER DRUGS

lthough designer drugs have appeared only in the last few decades, they are part of a long tradition of drug production and abuse throughout the world. Originally, all drugs were natural substances. Alcohol use is recorded in the writings of the earliest human civilizations more than 8,000 years ago. Use of narcotics made from plants dates back as far as 5000 B.C., when the juice of the poppy was cultivated to produce opium in the Middle Eastern region known as Mesopotamia (present-day Iraq). Use of marijuana was recorded 3,000 years ago in China and in early Hindu religious rites. Thousands of years before European settlers began to arrive in North and South America, the natives of those continents had discovered the pleasurable properties of coca leaves (from which cocaine is derived), peyote, and hallucinogenic mushrooms.

As drug use changed from medicinal or religious in orientation to more recreational use over the centuries, people started to become concerned with drug addiction. In the United States, the first wave of addiction to injectable narcotics came shortly after the invention of the hypodermic needle. Soldiers who had been wounded during the American Civil War (1861–65) were treated with the painkiller morphine (a derivative of opium); many became hopelessly addicted. In search of a drug with morphine's painkilling properties but not its addictive side effects, in 1898 the Bayer Company developed heroin. Unfortunately, this was soon found to be more addictive than morphine. These developments, combined with opium's unrestricted availability and an influx of opium-smoking immigrants from the Orient, contributed to a growing drug abuse problem in the United States during the late 19th and early 20th centuries.

In response, the federal government began imposing legal restrictions on drugs in the early part of the 20th century. The 1914 Harrison Act, which made nonmedical use of narcotics illegal, served to temporarily decrease widespread abuse of drugs. This attitude toward the danger of drugs extended even to alcohol, the most socially accepted drug. In the United States, alcohol use was banned for a 14-year period (called Prohibition) in the 1920s and early 1930s.

After World War II (1939–45), new drug problems began to emerge in the United States. Cocaine use had been virtually nonexistent for two decades, but drug addicts began appearing in prisons and at U.S. clinics. In addition, a synthetic drug, amphetamine (speed), was fast becoming popular on the streets. In the 1950s, Mexican opium made its way to New York, where it was refined into heroin and then distributed to major cities throughout the United States. During this period, federal narcotics agencies began to see an increase in addiction in major cities as well as an increasing number of young users. To stem the tide of abuse, both the Boggs Act of 1951 and the Narcotic Control Act of 1956 imposed harsh penalties and mandatory prison sentences for drug violations.

In the 1960s, drug use skyrocketed as America's youth began to question conventional values and institutions and to explore alternative lifestyles. The federal government responded with a tougher approach to fighting drugs. In 1966, the Bureau of Drug Abuse Control (BDAC), a predecessor of today's Drug Enforcement Administration (DEA), was created to control stimulants such as methamphetamine and various hallucinogens. Because of the crackdown on the traditional flow of illegal drugs, underground laboratories began making copycat drugs to satisfy demand on the street.

With the passage of the Controlled Substances Act (CSA) in 1970, possession of an illegal drug was made a misdemeanor, and intent to sell or transfer it a felony. The CSA also established five schedules that classify controlled substances according to their potential for abuse and legitimate medical value. These sweeping restrictions encouraged the emergence of even more illegal labs, where new drugs that would bypass the CSA could be made. The amateur chemists in these labs would create new substances that were different enough from controlled substances that they wouldn't violate the law, yet were close enough to produce many of the same effects as the original. The legal status of these designer drugs was short-lived, however, because between 1984 and 1986 they were also added to the list of controlled substances.

Drug use increased during the 1960s as teens and young adults began to explore alternative lifestyles. The Woodstock rock concert in August 1969 is seen as one of the highlights of this "hippie" movement.

Still, the separate ingredients needed to make the drugs could usually be purchased quite legally from a pharmacy, drugstore, or chemical supplier. Thus, the so-called "kitchen chemists" who created the drugs found a way to continue making their illegal products despite these new laws. It wasn't until 1988 that the Chemical Diversion and Trafficking Act placed regulations on the distribution, sale, import, and export of many of these chemicals, although some are still not restricted. Overall, the 1988 federal law, as well as similar state laws, has significantly cut into the availability of chemicals to the designer drug laboratory. Yet designer drugs continue to be manufactured and sold for profit.

Two police officials pour chunks of Ice (crystal methamphetamine) into boiling water to destroy the drug. Ice, which looks like clear crystal chunks that can be smoked, is sometimes called the "cocaine of the '90s."

METHAMPHETAMINE: A HISTORY

Amphetamine was first synthesized in 1887, and the related substance methamphetamine was developed approximately 30 years later. In 1931, the stimulant hit the commercial market as a nasal inhaler for the treatment of nasal congestion. Soon, however, the drug's popularity grew because of its additional effect of induced sleeplessness; it was seen as an "energy pill." In 1935, the first tablets that exploited this effect became available, and in the following years numerous claims for amphetamine's therapeutic uses emerged. In 1936, university students began taking the drug to help them stay awake while studying for exams. That prolonged alertness also made the drug popular among truck drivers, athletes, and soldiers during World War II.

Abuse of amphetamine sulfate (Benzedrine) and dextroamphetamine (Dexedrine) pills became widespread during the 1950s and 1960s. These pills were commonly prescribed by physicians, most often for weight loss; however, many were diverted to the illegal street market. During the 1960s, methamphetamine hydrochloride, known as "speed," was the most widely abused stimulant. High-intensity users, who became known as "speed freaks," would often inject the drug for days, until overcome by exhaustion or psychosis. Their aggressive behavior, volatile temper, and extreme weight loss gave rise to the once-familiar warning that "speed kills."

By the end of the 1960s, methamphetamine abuse began to wane. The pharmaceutical production had reached 10 billion tablets by 1970, when the Controlled Substances Act began strictly controlling the production, importation, and prescription of amphetamine and similar drugs. The Drug Enforcement Administration and medical licensing boards also cracked down on "script doctors" who freely handed out amphetamine prescriptions. As a result of the dwindling supply, illegal meth labs began popping up all over the western and southwestern United States. Since many of the labs were run by motorcycle gangs, disputes over control of the illegal methamphetamine market became responsible for the kind of gang-related violence once restricted to the cocaine trade.

Despite a roller-coaster methamphetamine market ever since, the late 1990s have seen the drug's popularity surge once again, but this time in the smokable form Ice. Although domestic suppliers still operate, organized crime groups in Mexico appear responsible for the latest increase in production on both sides of the border.

MDMA: A HISTORY

Merck, a German chemical company, developed MDMA as a diet pill in 1912, although there's no evidence that it was ever sold as such. The drug was ignored until the 1960s, when its use was first reported in the United States. In 1965, MDMA was re-created by an American chemist named Alexander Shulgin, who shared his work with a small group of psychiatrists. They began experimenting with MDMA, using it during psychotherapy to enhance openness, awareness, and empathy. The psychiatrists compared the drug's effects to Adam's innocent and blissful state in the biblical Garden of Eden, before he ate the forbidden fruit. For this reason, they nicknamed the drug "Adam."

In the early 1980s, some small drug manufacturers learned of the euphoric feelings caused by MDMA and started producing it for recreational use. By this time, MDMA had already earned its more popular street name, Ecstasy. Word about Ecstasy spread, and it began popping up on college campuses and in nightclubs throughout the country. At the time, Ecstasy was not yet restricted by the federal government, so its use was still legal. Then, in 1985, the Drug Enforcement Administration banned MDMA under the Controlled Substances Act (CSA). Because tests had shown that MDMA might cause brain damage in humans, MDMA was placed on CSA's Schedule I—the most restrictive category of illegal drugs. Due to their highly addictive nature and a lack of medical uses, it is illegal to make, possess, or sell any Schedule I drug in the United States.

Despite its illegal status, Ecstasy is widely used today at raves and in night clubs throughout Australia, Great Britain, and the United States. In fact, Ecstasy and electronic music are credited with inspiring the rave dance culture—it's said that the combination of the drug and the music help to create a trancelike state for ravers who want to dance all night. Recently, in New York, it also has become the drug of choice for young people in the alternative music scene.

PHENCYCLIDINE (PCP): A HISTORY

Phencyclidine was first manufactured as a pain-relieving medication in 1957 by Parke-Davis Laboratories, a pharmaceutical company. At the time, it was considered safer than any other painkiller on the market. However, although it worked well, nearly 20 percent of the patients awoke after surgery having hallucinations and acting extremely agitated; some even had seizures or epileptic fits. As a result, medical use of PCP in humans was discontinued in 1965, and it was marketed to veterinarians strictly as an animal tranquilizer (it apparently didn't produce such nasty side effects in animals). But even veterinarians stopped using phencyclidine in 1978, and all PCP manufactured since 1979 has been done so illegally.

During the 1960s, the drug subculture in New York and San Francisco discovered PCP and nicknamed it the "peace pill." But the drug's popularity rapidly waned as users experienced "bad trips" and unexpected reactions following its use. In the late 1960s and early 1970s, PCP emerged as a frequent contaminant of other drugs sold on the street,

Pills seized in a police raid. Designer drugs were initially produced in the 1980s to provide users a "high" that was not illegal under the Controlled Substances Act (CSA).

most often in samples of hallucinogens and THC. The Drug Enforcement Administration reports that abuse of the drug resurfaced from 1975 into the late 1980s because of the low price and powerful effects. An especially sharp increase in PCP trafficking occurred between 1981 and 1985, particularly among teenagers. Since the mid-1980s, narcotics agencies have reported that the number of PCP laboratories seized has been considerably smaller than that reported in 1978. Still, in the past few years, demand for PCP has once again risen and the drug has reappeared as a contaminant in other street drugs.

FENTANYL: A HISTORY

First synthesized in Belgium in 1968, fentanyl was introduced into clinical practice in the 1960s as an intravenous anesthetic for heart surgery, a function it still serves. Since the mid-1970s, illegal use of pharmaceutical fentanyl in the medical community has been a problem in the United States.

Around the same time, underground laboratories began manufacturing fentanyl derivatives that mimicked the effects of heroin and morphine. Addicts who could no longer afford heroin began switching to these cheaper and more readily available designer drugs. China White, which first appeared in Orange County, California, in 1979, became notorious as the first synthetically produced fentanyl to cause a fatal overdose. In fact, much of the history of designer fentanyl reads like a morgue report. Between 1980 and 1985, China White and several other fentanyl derivatives were responsible for 100 unintentional overdose deaths in California. In 1991, the fentanyl drug nicknamed Tango and Cash was implicated in at least 28 deaths, primarily in New York and other areas in the northeast. The following year, China White was found to be the cause of death in 21 overdoses over the course of two months in Philadelphia. To date, fentanyl derivatives are responsible for the drug overdose deaths of nearly 200 people in the United States.

In 1982, China White was placed on Schedule I of the Controlled Substances Act (CSA), along with other drugs that have the highest potential for abuse and have no recognized legitimate medical use.

MEPERIDINE (MPPP): A HISTORY

Introduced as a potent pain reliever in the 1930s, meperidine was considered an opioid—a synthetic substitute for opiates, like heroin, that is not derived from the opium poppy. Abuse of the drug was first reported in 1976, when a 23-year-old graduate student in Washington, D.C., was referred to the National Institute of Mental Health because of Parkinson's disease symptoms. Parkinson's disease is a nervous system disorder that can paralyze its victims. The student was a self-admitted addict, who had been making and injecting what he thought was MPPP

A computer-generated image of the molecules of Ecstasy. The drug, initially created as a diet pill, became widely known during the 1980s.

at home. However, in attempting to synthesize the drug he had mistakenly made the poisonous by-product MPTP.

According to the Drug Enforcement Administration, MPPP became more popular on the black market in the early 1980s. Along with it, MPTP began appearing more frequently among street users, especially on the West Coast. In 1982, a California chemist working on an illegal version of the prescription painkiller Demerol took a shortcut that backfired. Once it hit the street, users began showing up at hospital emergency wards with signs of Parkinson's disease. By 1985, the Centers for Disease Control (CDC) had identified approximately 400 individuals who appeared, because of their telltale Parkinson's symptoms, to have been exposed to MPTP. There were probably many more who were never seen by the CDC or other government agencies.

Despite the dangers, labs continued to make MPPP and the number of users increased. The only difference, Dr. William Langston reported to the U.S. Senate at a hearing in July 1985, seemed to be that many of the underground formulas, which had been copied and circulated many times, now had a notice at the bottom of the page—"Warning, if made improperly or carelessly, this can damage your clients"—with a page attached describing the symptoms of Parkinson's disease. Of course, the profit-driven labs didn't slow down production until demand for meperidine finally reached a plateau in the 1990s. Largely because of its life-threatening consequences and also due to the availability of other heroin substitutes, MPPP's popularity has since waned. But it is still on the street and users are still showing up in hospital emergency wards.

GHB: A HISTORY

GHB was originally developed in the early 1960s as a medication to promote sleep before surgery. It was considered to be a low-risk drug, leading many researchers to explore other potential uses for the substance. In Europe, GHB's medical applications included use as a general anesthetic, a treatment for insomnia and narcolepsy, an aid to childbirth (by increasing strength of contractions and decreasing pain), and a treatment for alcohol withdrawal syndrome.

Starting in the 1980s, GHB could be purchased at health food stores. Bodybuilders favored the substance because they believed that by mixing the powder in water they could strip away fat while promoting muscle growth. Soon word got out that GHB produced euphoria and increased sensitivity to touch, thereby appealing to people looking for a legal alternative to Ecstasy. It was even hyped as an aphrodisiac.

The Food and Drug Administration (FDA) declared GHB illegal in 1990 after 57 cases of GHB-induced illnesses (ranging from nausea and vomiting to respiratory problems, seizures, and comas) were reported to poison control centers and emergency rooms. With similar reports continuing to come in from all areas of the country, the FDA classified it as a Schedule I drug the following year. As a result, GHB use was restricted to licensed researchers only, and possession or sale of it became a misdemeanor. Despite such legal restrictions, homemade versions of GHB became increasingly popular. However, since the fall of 1996, the drug has been implicated in several deaths, causing many to think twice before using it.

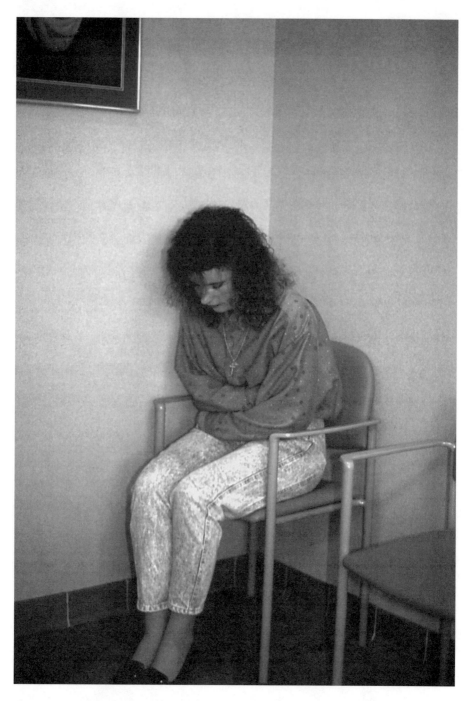

The pressures of growing up and assuming new responsibilities can drive a person to try drugs as a means of escape.

3

WHY DO TEENS USE DRUGS?

Many teens never feel compelled to try drugs. Some experiment once or twice, but don't like it enough to do it again or to try other drugs. Others use drugs for years and eventually stop. Then there are those who become hopelessly addicted, letting drugs control—and in many cases, destroy—their lives.

So, *why* do they use drugs? Curiosity is what drives most teens to try drugs for the first time. Teens may hear stories in school or from friends about how a particular drug will make them feel strong, confident, sexy, or smarter. A person's perception regarding the risk of drug use is also critical. If young adults are not informed about the dangers of drugs—if they view them as "harmless"—they are more inclined to experiment. Surprisingly, methamphetamine is regarded by most teens as a drug that carries with it little or no risk of addiction or death. In fact, national studies on drug use among adolescents have found that since 1991 the percentage of teens associating great risk with meth use has declined considerably. Meanwhile, use of methamphetamine by teens is on the rise.

Some teens experiment with drugs to feel independent or to experience something novel and exciting. Others may turn to drugs as a means of coping with the pressures of adolescence. They just want to fit in, so they do what everyone else is doing. Maybe they believe that drugs will help them separate from their anxious, insecure selves and make them into more desirable people.

There are those who resort to drugs as a way to handle, or block out, psychological or family problems. If teens feel that they have no one to turn to for help, they may seek some solace in the high that drugs promise. This is often because they've watched their parents or other family members "handle" difficulty with drugs. After the high wears off, however, they're still confronted with the same problems—and maybe more severe ones.

Peer pressure, and a teen's living environment, can affect drug use. A person whose friends use drugs, or who grows up surrounded by others who abuse drugs, is more likely to start using than a person who does not have these same influences.

So, what separates those who simply experiment from those who go on to abuse drugs? Numerous theories about the cause of drug abuse exist, but most researchers agree that no single factor can be blamed. Rather, one person may be more likely than another to abuse drugs because of a combination of influences in his or her life.

WHO'S AT HIGHER RISK AND WHY?

Apparently, biology plays a part, as users are more often male than female and usually hang around with friends who use drugs. Again, using methamphetamine as an example, a 1997 study conducted by the National Institute on Drug Abuse found that 64 percent of regular meth users (those who have used it at least once in the last month) in the United States are male and that the majority are under 20 years old. Teens who regularly use drugs tend to have unconventional beliefs and attitudes, and are often hyperactive and sensation seekers. Typically, they perform below average in school, in part due to their frequent absences, and have low educational aspirations overall.

Some teens who use drugs may feel that their parents don't love them enough; others may not feel very attached to their parents. A common problem among teen drug users is a lack of consistent supervision and discipline from their parents. These same parents are also likely to use and abuse alcohol or other drugs themselves. Teen users are usually less involved than nonusers in church or community groups, which could offer them drug-free ways to spend their times. And they often live in troubled neighborhoods, where they may suffer from depression or emotional distress.

Peer influence is an important factor in beginning drug use; 65 percent of respondents in a 1995 survey on drug use published in the *American Journal on Addictions* attributed their initiation to alcohol and drugs to peer influence. More than half the respondents were first given alcohol or drugs by a friend. Peers influenced these children either directly through pressure or because alcohol and drug use seemed to be a direct path to the in-crowd. In general, teenagers are trying to break out of childhood and assert themselves as independent and in control. Such growth means greater exploration and sensation seeking, as reflected in the more than 20 percent of respondents who identified curiosity and fun as reasons for first use.

Another important factor is parental attitudes. The way that parents view, and behave toward, legal and illegal drug use can heavily influence an adolescent's decision to experiment with drugs. If parents smoke cigarettes and regularly drink alcohol, then their children are likely to view these substances, and perhaps drugs in general, as attractive. It's been

Close family relationships make it less likely that a young adult will turn to drugs.

found that if parents use medically prescribed tranquilizers, their children are likely to be more interested in trying drugs in general. Through their use of prescription drugs, parents may set the example that drugs can be used to handle psychological problems. Their children, in turn, may use drugs to handle their own feelings of psychological distress. They've learned a dangerous habit: self-medication.

MOVING FROM USE TO ABUSE

Although teens tend to begin sampling alcohol around 12 years old, and drugs a year or two later, there are those who may start earlier. Difficulty or boredom in school may contribute to such use. Of concern is that the earlier the age of initial experimentation with alcohol and drugs, the more likely the person will use them more heavily at a later age. Beyond the usual adolescent sampling, early problems with drinking or alcoholism, especially before the age of 15, are also associated with increased risk of drug abuse and dependence.

WHO'S LESS LIKELY TO USE?

That depends. A boy who doesn't do very well in school and whose parents use drugs appears to be a likely user—but he also may have high self-esteem and be very active in community and church groups. The latter are factors that may help him be strong in resisting the lure of illegal drugs. A teenager's personality and character, living conditions, and environment can mean the difference between healthy resilience and shaky vulnerability to dangerous drug use. Each person is different.

Having close relationships with parents and family members, as well as having parents who do not suffer from drinking or drug problems, are certainly healthy signs. Interestingly, being female seems to reduce the risk of drug abuse, as girls are less likely than boys to use drugs in the first place. But many still do. Teens who are strong academic achievers and have high aspirations for their future tend to spend their time more constructively. And those who have a strong religious faith and close supportive relationships with people outside their family are more likely to resist abusing drugs. Overall, high self-esteem and independence, creativity, and temperament are individual characteristics that can overcome even the most difficult odds.

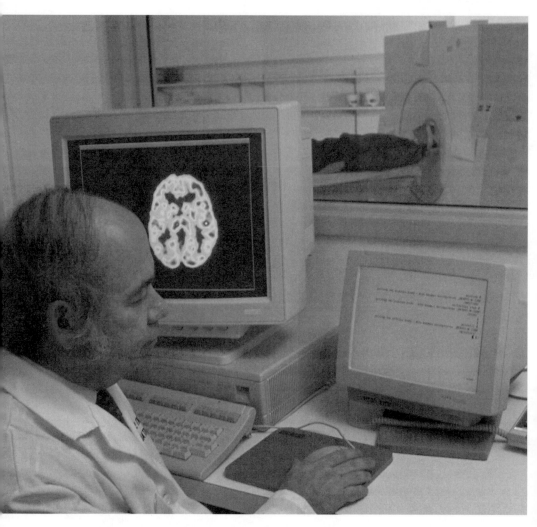

A doctor examines a computer indicator of a person whose brain is being scanned. Researchers have found that use of drugs can cause permanent changes to the brain and other body systems.

4

HOW ARE USERS AFFECTED?

Naturally, a person's reaction to drugs depends on which drug he or she takes. But it is also greatly affected by how much is taken at one time, the method used to take the drug, and whether or not alcohol or other drugs are taken with it. Individual characteristics—such as the user's previous drug experiences and his or her psychological and emotional stability—play a major role in determining whether that sought-after high or a deadly low is reached. Where and with whom a person takes the drug can mean the difference between a good trip and a bad trip.

These are all factors over which the user has some control. But there are other influences that make the reaction totally unpredictable. Too often, the person does not know beforehand the actual contents of the drug. For instance, although a tablet may look like Ecstasy, it may have been cut with caffeine, speed, baking soda, or more dangerous ingredients. Doses of China White might be cut with a laxative, strychnine (a rat poison that acts as a stimulant on the central nervous system), or heroin. The unpredictability of such contaminants is precisely what makes illegal drugs so risky.

A drug's content can be so deadly that even a first-time user could be risking not only a bad experience, but possibly his or her life as well. However, the people who are in greatest danger are those who use drugs excessively and frequently. Such sustained use can ruin a person's life. For example, drug use may lead to psychological problems that start with disturbing flashbacks and paranoia and can eventually move on to depression, mood swings, and delirium. Worse, the user may end up with psychosis, a frightening loss of contact with reality that makes it nearly impossible to function in school, at work, and in social situations. Once psychosis is triggered, it is difficult to treat. In many cases, the user may have been unaware that he or she had a preexisting psychiatric problem until drug use brought out into the open.

When a person takes a lot of methamphetamine over a short period of time (a "binge"), the drug user may fall into a period of agitation and depression, known as the "crash."

THE EFFECTS OF METHAMPHETAMINE

A person's immediate reaction to speed or crystal meth depends largely on how it is taken. Within seconds of smoking or injecting methamphetamine, the user experiences an intense, pleasurable rush that lasts only a few minutes. Snorting the drug will produce a euphoric high within about 5 minutes, but not the intense rush. Swallowing produces the same high as snorting, but it takes a longer (up to 15 to 20 minutes) for the effects to kick in. A methamphetamine high can last anywhere from a few hours up to a day, depending on how much is used.

At lower doses, methamphetamine makes a person feel energetic, alert, self-confident, even powerful. At the same time, meth's appetite-suppressing qualities mean the user probably won't want to eat or sleep because of all the energy she or he has. A bad reaction might cause a user's body to writhe and jerk, and arms and legs to flail about. The person may become irritable, confused, and overly anxious. Depending on the situation, many users may become aggressive, some to the point of violence.

In addition to the possible complications caused by speed, smokable Ice can create even more problems. Distorted vision is common, with some users hallucinating about themselves and others around them. Ice might also interfere with a person's judgment, hamper physical coordination, and slow down reflexes. Of greater concern is the effect Ice can have on internal organs, including heart palpitations, brain damage, and lung and liver problems.

Regular use of methamphetamine can lead to serious medical conditions. Because meth increases the user's heart rate and blood pressure, it can sometimes cause irreversible damage to blood vessels in the brain, producing strokes. The drug can also cause severe convulsions. Chest pain and hypertension are signs of heart problems, which could progress to a heart attack and death.

As a person continues to use the drug, he or she must take greater amounts to experience the same pleasurable feelings because his or her body has become used to the drug's effects. This change is called "tolerance." Users often become agitated and feel "wired," and behave unpredictably. They may be friendly and calm one moment, angry and terrified the next. Some feel compelled to repeat meaningless tasks, such as taking apart and reassembling bits of machinery. Others may pick at imaginary insects or parasites on their skin.

After a number of days of binging on methamphetamine, usually without sleeping or eating, a user becomes too tired to continue or runs out of meth, and stops taking the drug. This leads to a "crash" that can last a few days. Initially, the crash makes the user agitated and depressed, sometimes with the urge for more methamphetamine. But these feelings soon give way to lethargy, followed by a long, deep sleep. Once the user awakens, however, the depression returns and may last for days—a time when the potential for suicide is high.

Over a long period of time, high doses of meth may cause "stimulant psychosis," which completely alters the user's personality. In fact, the more someone takes meth, the more his or her personality will change. Even weekly use can make a person colder, more aggressive, and paranoid. Users may become psychotic—feeling intensely paranoid, hearing voices, and experiencing bizarre delusions (believing, for example, that other people are talking about or following them).

Methamphetamine-induced panic and psychosis can be very danger-ous and can lead to violence or suicide. It is not unusual for psychosis to persist for days after the last dose of methamphetamine. Indeed, there are many reports of users remaining paranoid, delusional, apathetic, and socially withdrawn for weeks. Occasionally, methamphetamine-related psychosis lasts for years. But experts believe that in these cases, the drug has probably triggered symptoms of a preexisting mental disorder.

THE EFFECTS OF ECSTASY

Because much of the Ecstasy sold on the street is not pure, its effect on users can be totally unpredictable. Dealers who sell Ecstasy often cut it with other substances, such as cold medicine, PCP, or rat poison, to increase their profits. Ecstasy that has been laced with LSD can cause the person to hallucinate for up to 12 hours—a very scary experience for someone who's not expecting it. Mixing Ecstasy with speed can cause users to overheat dangerously, especially at crowded raves where they may be dancing for hours. Use of other drugs with Ecstasy can also have detrimental effects. For example, drinking alcohol with Ecstasy puts a lot of stress on the liver and can lead to intense dehydration.

Within 20 minutes to an hour of taking pure Ecstasy, some users claim to feel euphoric, while others maintain that an all-over pleasant,

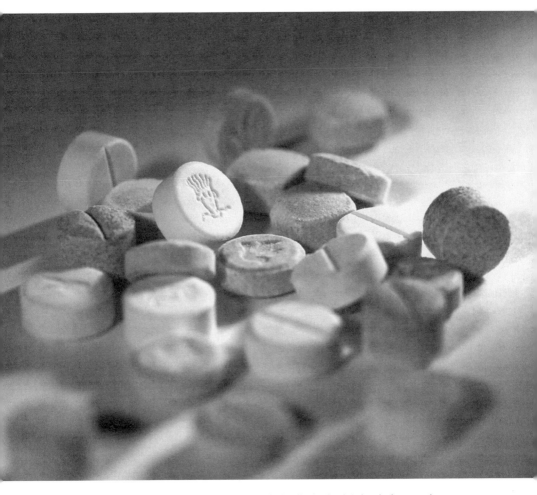

One of the most serious effects of Ecstasy is a depletion in the brain's level of serotonin, a neurotransmitter that affects behavior, mood, and thinking ability. Long-term users may find their personality permanently changed by the drug.

happy feeling is more accurate. That initial feeling of intense emotion is what gave the drug the street name of Ecstasy. At first energetic and confident, users soon feel calm and carefree—feelings that generally last about two to three hours. Some users say that Ecstasy enables them to be more expressive and outgoing, making them want to talk and smile a lot or to hug everyone. Ecstasy also heightens all five senses, making a simple act like running your fingers through your hair feel intensely pleasurable.

That's one of the reasons Ecstasy is so popular at raves. With nonstop music, light-and-video shows, and throngs of dancers, raves indulge the senses and satisfy a user's desire to feel close to others.

But users can encounter many problems with Ecstasy. Physically, a person's heart starts beating faster as blood pressure increases. Muscles can become tense, teeth involuntarily clench, and the user is likely to get the chills or break into a sweat. Other debilitating effects include nausea, faintness, and blurred vision. The day after using Ecstasy, some people experience a "hangover" that keeps them abnormally awake despite feelings of fatigue and drowsiness, throws off their balance, and leaves them with headaches and sore jaw muscles from all that teeth-clenching the night before.

In addition to bad physical reactions, a person can also experience psychological problems while high on Ecstasy, according to the *Diagnostic and Statistical Manual of Mental Disorders*, fourth edition (*DSM*-IV), the standard reference work on psychological disorders. A user may hallucinate or become confused, resulting in panic and paranoia. Someone could fall into a deep depression or suffer severe anxiety, especially if depressed or stressed out before taking Ecstasy. Some users' reactions have had dangerous consequences, such as jumping out of a window under the belief that they can fly, although such extreme behavior is often linked to a preexisting mental disorder.

The likelihood of negative reactions increases the more a person takes Ecstasy. In fact, over time users develop a tolerance to the drug's euphoric effects, and they feel only agitation after extended use. Such diminishing returns can cause some to give up on Ecstasy, while it leads others to continue trying greater and greater amounts of the drug in an effort to recapture the initial feelings it caused. These are the users who risk serious psychological damage.

Use of MDMA causes serious long-term consequences. Ecstasy depletes a very important chemical in the brain, serotonin, which affects mood, sleeping and eating habits, thinking processes, aggressive behavior, sexual function, and sensitivity to pain. While one-time users usually distort their serotonin levels only temporarily, heavy users may be risking brain damage that remains long after the high has worn off. If the brain can't compensate for the changes caused by the drug, the long-term effects could include increased aggression, severe depression, and even suicide.

Studies conducted at Johns Hopkins University used positron emission tomography (PET) scanners, which can produce detailed images of active areas of the brain, to study two groups of recreational drug users. The first group used Ecstasy and other drugs; the others used drugs other than Ecstasy. Although all the drug users showed reduced brain function when compared to nonusers, only the Ecstasy users showed deficiencies in all brain regions. Though the effects of such changes could take years or even decades to show up, they have potentially serious consequences for the regular Ecstasy users who take one or two tablets every weekend.

THE EFFECTS OF PHENCYCLIDINE (PCP)

PCP's effects can be felt soon after the user takes the drug, and the length of the high is never the same: it can last from a few hours to a few days. Like the duration of the drug's effects, the feelings caused by PCP can be totally unpredictable. For some, the drug acts as a stimulant, speeding up body functions. For others, it's a hallucinogen that causes them to have out-of-body experiences in which they perceive themselves and those around them in a very distorted way. Many users feel a heightened sense of power. While some feel relaxed and intensely happy on PCP, others feel threatened and—because of fear, anxiety, or panic—may behave violently. Feeling spaced out and having a difficult time interacting with people is very common. PCP may also release hidden emotional or mental problems. Differences in the response to PCP may be dose-related or based on the individual response of the user. Most regular users admit to having had at least one "bad trip," but the hope of achieving the extraordinary high that PCP can bring is powerful enough to keep them coming back for more.

The problem is that bad trips are sometimes fatal. Some deaths have been directly linked to PCP overdoses. Others have been caused by the drug's psychological impact, which has lead to accidents, violence, and suicides. People may imagine that they are being attacked by an animal or insects. When this happens, they begin fighting or running. They may injure others while trying to get away from whatever they believe is after them. Users have been known to jump out of windows several stories high to escape such hallucinations. In some cases, people high on PCP have continued fighting or running even after they've been shot or lost an arm. During periods of extreme anxiety or disorientation,

PCP is commonly added to other drugs, such as marijuana joints, to increase their potency. However, this combination of drugs can cause unexpected reactions in the user, such as hallucinations, violence, or suicidal tendencies.

some users may become aggressive, while others may withdraw and have difficulty communicating. Taking large amounts of PCP can also cause death from repeated convulsions, heart and lung failure, or ruptured blood vessels in the brain.

At low doses, the physical effects of PCP include shallow and rapid breathing, increased blood pressure and heart rate, and a marked rise in body temperature that leads to profuse sweating. Many users feel a general numbness in their arms and legs. Their speech can be random and garbled.

At higher doses, blood pressure, heart rate, and breathing level drop rapidly. This can lead to dizziness, nausea, and vomiting. Because the drug depresses the central nervous system, which controls these functions, taking it with other depressant drugs, such as alcohol, can lead to coma or accidental overdose. The user's vision may be distorted, causing him or her to flick the eyes up and down uncontrollably. A profound decrease in awareness of pain can put the user in life-threatening situations. Muscles may contract so intensely that they cause jerky, uncoordinated movements and bizarre postures. Some users feel hostile and paranoid and become preoccupied with death.

Little is known about PCP's long-term effects. Some users suffer unpleasant "flashbacks," which are unpredictable, spontaneous recurrences of the original PCP trip without the user's having taken the drug again. Flashbacks can occur weeks, months, even a year after the last encounter with the drug. Typically they last only a few minutes and are usually visual images ranging from formless colors to frightening hallucinations. Teens who use PCP may be warping their learning ability as well as their hormonal activity related to physical growth and development. After prolonged use of PCP, some users have suffered persistent speech problems and loss of memory, especially of recent events. Others have ended up with severe, long-lasting anxiety, depression, and social withdrawal.

One of the most serious effects of PCP use is symptoms of a psychological disorder called schizophrenia. This mental disease causes a person to lose touch with reality, changes his or her personality, and makes its victim unable to function in everyday life. Use of phencyclidine causes similar symptoms, called a PCP psychosis. This temporary disturbance of the thought processes may last for days or weeks. For years, PCP psychosis has been compared to schizophrenia because of the similarity in behavior patterns. Hallucinations and delusional thinking are common both in PCP users and in schizophrenics.

Research is under way to decipher how PCP causes symptoms of schizophrenia, and this, scientists hope, will help researchers learn more about the mental disorder and how to cure or prevent it. Other research has shown that PCP can have beneficial effects. PCP has been found to protect the brain from permanent damage after a stroke or heart attack. Basic brain research on the actions of amino acids and the effects of commonly abused drugs led to the discovery that PCP can stop the uncontrolled activity that destroys nerve cells. This discovery is expected to help people who suffer from any trauma that interrupts the supply of oxygen to the brain. However, PCP's side effects make it ineffective in medical treatment, and researchers are now looking for drugs that can work like PCP without producing the psychological effects.

THE EFFECTS OF FENTANYL

Designer drugs that are based on fentanyl are 80 to 100 times more potent than heroin, depending on how they are made, and 200 times more potent than morphine. They also take effect in the user very rapidly, typically within only a few minutes. Because of the potency and quick onset, even a very small dose of a pure fentanyl derivative can lead to sudden death. That's why drugs like China White have to be cut with some substance to weaken their effects.

Often called synthetic heroin, China White is made to duplicate the euphoric effects of that opiate. Unfortunately, just as with heroin, China White is so addictive that a large percentage of the people who try it end up hooked. After injecting the drug, users feel a brief rush of euphoria followed by an overall calmness. Some users get an immediate burning sensation in their arm. Thereafter their breathing slows, causing the oxygen level in their blood to become dangerously low—which means that they are in danger of heart failure and possible death. China White can also cause muscles to become painfully hard and rigid. Users generally feel these effects for about 30 minutes to a couple of hours, depending on how the drug was made.

After prolonged use of China White, users tend to experience severe and painful constipation, which is why the drug is sometimes cut with a mild laxative. Many of the illegal labs also add in much more harmful substances—like antihistamines or strychnine—to increase their profits. Unfortunately, those ingredients can also cause a deadly overdose. Even after trying China White once, a person may start uncontrollably

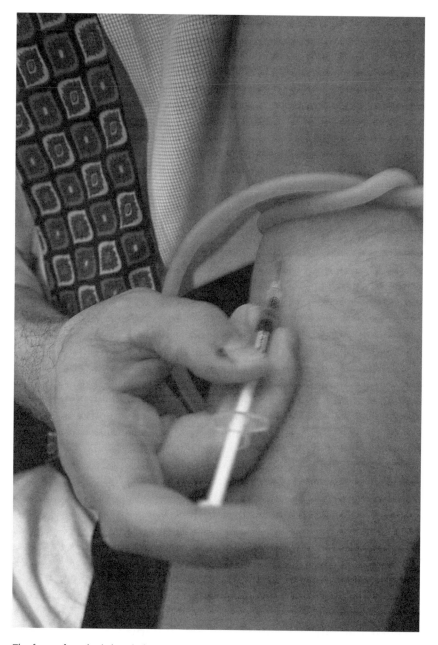

The form of synthetic heroin known as China White is so potent that users have died of overdoses immediately after injecting the drug.

shaking their arms, legs, and head. But for regular users, this can develop into a permanent condition. In addition, some users become permanently paralyzed or disabled.

Addiction to synthetic heroin combines both a psychological dependence and a physical dependence on the drug. Psychological dependence means that the drug user has a powerful desire to use the drug, even if there is no physical need to do so. However, with opioid users there is a physical need, because the person's body has become so used to the drug that unpleasant physical symptoms will occur if it is withdrawn suddenly.

Fentanyl and other opioids cause physical dependence because they change the way that the brain works. When the drug enters a user's bloodstream, opioid molecules attach themselves to certain parts of the brain, called receptors, as well as to the neurons of the central nervous system. The binding together of the opioid and the receptor produces an electrical charge in the nervous system that causes feelings of pleasure.

The reason that opioids can link to areas of the human brain is that they mimic the effects of substances produced naturally in the body called endorphins. Endorphins are protein compounds that are produced in the human pituitary gland and released into the bloodstream constantly, often in response to outside stimuli. These proteins are neurotransmitters, meaning that they affect the neurological messages from the nervous system to the brain and help regulate responses to internal and external events such as stress, pain, or excitement. Endorphins have been called "the brain's own natural painkillers" and may contribute to euphoric feelings such as the "runner's high" experienced after prolonged exercise.

However, the human neurological system is very complicated and very delicate, and drugs overload the system with false messages. When fentanyl or synthetic heroin is injected into the body, the level of these pleasure-causing opioids is far greater than the human body's endorphin system can handle. As a result, the body is tricked by the high level of artificial endorphins introduced by the drug and stops producing endorphins naturally. When the drug's effects wear off, painful symptoms result because the body no longer produces its own painkilling endorphins. This is called withdrawal. The signs of opioid withdrawal can include severe muscle cramps, nausea, convulsions, and hallucinations. Withdrawal can be so unpleasant that the user will continue to take the drug just to avoid it.

THE EFFECTS OF MEPERIDINE (MPPP)

Meperidine, like fentanyl, is a synthetic opiate, or opioid, so it shares many of the painkilling narcotic effects of other opioids, such as the natural drugs morphine and heroin, and synthetic opioids. These drugs cause people to feel drowsy, warm, and content. They also relieve stress and discomfort by creating a relaxed detachment from pain, desires, and activity. As well as killing pain, moderate doses of pure opioids produce a range of mild effects. They depress, or slow, the activity of the body's central nervous system, affecting such reflexes as coughing, breathing, and heart rate. They also cause widening of the blood vessels, which gives the feeling of warmth.

Soon after taking the drug, the user experiences a pleasant surge of feelings through his or her body, known as the rush. In a few minutes, these intense feelings fade, and are followed by a few hours of gradually decreasing sensation, usually accompanied by feelings of sleepiness or lethargy.

Because opioids act on the nervous symptom, a user's pulse and breathing rates are slowed and his or her blood pressure drops. The physical symptoms of someone who is high on MPPP include poor coordination, slurred speech, and slowed reactions. Many users have had difficulty speaking and swallowing after taking MPPP. Some who've taken it orally say that the drug leaves a metallic or medicinal taste in the mouth.

If MPPP is taken in conjunction with other "depressant" drugs such as alcohol, or with another opioid, the user risks an overdose that could result in a coma or even death. Another dangerous effect of taking MPPP occurs when the drug is produced carelessly in an illegal laboratory. It is very easy for a careless amateur chemist to produce the toxic substance MPTP. If this is taken, a variety of health problems can result, including permanent brain damage and, in some cases, death.

It's precisely because of such deadly experiences that meperidine has been in and out of favor on the streets since it was introduced in the 1970s. Users want the heroinlike rush and lingering high, but

When MPPP is synthesized in illegal, underground labs, there is a danger that an inexperienced chemist may accidentally create the by-product MPTP. This toxic substance may then be distributed as MPPP; however, it can cause brain damage with effects that resemble Parkinson's disease—uncontrollable shaking of limbs and loss of memory—as well as other health problems.

they fear the many risks. An error in the production process can have irreversible, even deadly, consequences for the user. When a lab gets sloppy and inadvertently produces MPTP, that's when users have the most to fear.

A person who takes MPTP often exhibits the symptoms of Parkinson's disease. This progressive neurological condition is commonly marked by an uncontrollable trembling of the hands or other extremities, even when the patient is at rest. Parkinson's is characterized by a loss of cognitive ability (for example, loss of memory, reduced ability to calculate or use higher thought processes, and lack of judgment regarding surroundings). This is called dementia.

Other reactions to the dangerous by-product MPTP range from sudden jerking of the arms, legs, and head to freezing of the muscles so that the user can barely move. A person can usually tell when MPTP has been injected because of a fiery burning sensation in the veins. These symptoms can occur the very first time someone uses a botched batch of MPPP, and by that point it's already too late.

THE EFFECTS OF GAMMA-HYDROXYBUTYRIC ACID (GHB)

Relaxed and feeling drunk, but at the same time clear-headed and with no hangover—that's the way many users describe a GHB high. At small doses, GHB lowers social inhibitions, in a way similar to alcohol, and increases sexual desire. Higher doses can result in general numbness with respiratory depression and coma. The problem is determining whether you're actually taking a small or a large dose, much of which depends on body weight and individual sensitivity. But it also depends on drug potency, something the user cannot know until it may be too late. Since it's made in illegal laboratories, GHB is no more reliable than any other designer drug. However, the effects of GHB are particularly sensitive to dosage level, with small increases in the amount causing significantly stronger effects. Therefore, someone may think they're taking a small dose, only to overdose because the batch was highly concentrated, as the following story illustrates:

> While sitting around talking with her friends, Gina drank small amounts from a friend's bottle of GHB. As she felt the effects wear off, she decided to drink some more. This time, she drank from a different bottle. Remembering she had drunk four capfuls from the first bottle, she decided she'd be safe taking half as much (two capfuls) the second time. Unfortunately, doses from the second bottle were much stronger than the first, so she accidentally ingested more than her body could handle.

People who use GHB in combination with alcohol are at an especially high risk for a deadly overdose.

Gina began to feel woozy and dizzy within a half hour and from that point remembered very little. The next morning her friends told her that they had seen her becoming unsteady. Then, she had started to vomit before passing out on the floor. They tried moving her to make her more comfortable, but she continued to throw up. Finally, they brought her to the hospital, where she remained unconscious for several hours. When she awoke, extremely dehydrated and with severe head pains, she had no idea where she was. Once her blood pressure, heart rate, and other vital signs had returned to normal, the hospital released her. Gina had overdosed, but she was lucky to walk away with nothing more than a severe hangover for a couple of days.

GHB normally tastes very salty, something like baking soda. Improperly manufactured GHB can also contain contaminants that may be poisonous and have a more caustic taste. The toxic chemicals used in the synthesis of GHB may cause chemical burns to the esophagus, mouth, and throat. When combined with alcohol and other drugs, the potential for deadly overdoses escalates rapidly. Numerous overdoses in Texas and nationwide have required emergency room treatment and mechanical breathing assistance.

A low dose of GHB often causes effects similar to those of one to three drinks of alcohol, depending on a person's size. Users will typically feel the effects within 10 to 15 minutes, and they become stronger after about a half hour. A GHB high can last for several hours. In addition to the mild relaxation and increased sociability, users may also feel mildly dizzy and have difficulty walking normally. A slightly higher dose increases the relaxing effects and the dizziness. Some users maintain that they find music, dancing, and talking much more enjoyable at this dosage level. Also similar to the effects of alcohol, users tend to slur their speech, act silly, and be increasingly incoherent on GHB.

But it's not all a party, even at low doses. Minute increases in dose can markedly increase feelings of nausea and grogginess. Many users also suffer reactions ranging from delusions and depression to amnesia and liver failure. Unfortunately, in the search for the optimal amount, a user can accidentally go from low dose to overdose in a matter of minutes.

One reason that GHB has become so popular as a club drug is that some people experience extremely positive feelings on heavy doses of GHB. However, higher levels may not only heighten the good feelings, but also worsen the bad. Users can lose almost all sense of balance and run the risk of seizures. Dizziness can plummet to unconsciousness and nausea can turn to body-racking vomiting. An overdose can start out as a strong drowsy feeling with irregular and depressed breathing that deepens into prolonged unconsciousness or a coma that lasts for hours. If a person begins vomiting while unconscious, he or she could suffocate and die. Even a small amount of GHB can be lethal if combined with alcohol. Of the relatively few deaths in the United States that have been attributed to GHB, most have involved alcohol or other drugs.

Studies have found that drug use can lead to violence and increased criminal activity. Certain drugs, like PCP, seem to cause their users to become violent.

5

THE IMPACT ON SOCIETY

A recent study of over 7,600 junior high and high school students (grades 7 to 12) from 53 schools in New York State served to reaffirm many previous studies of adolescent drug use (Kandel and Davies, 1996). Alcohol and cigarettes were the most frequently used drugs, used by 84 percent and 52 percent, respectively, of the students studied. The most common illicit drug was marijuana, used by 28 percent of the students. Nearly one-fifth of the students (18 percent) reported ever having used an illicit drug other than marijuana, many of which were designer drugs. Stimulants had been used by 11 percent, followed by inhalants and cocaine in any form (6 percent each), and psychedelics or hallucinogens (5 percent).

In the United States, drug use has increased dramatically over the past three decades. In 1962, approximately 4 million Americans had ever used an illicit drug; by 1992, that number had climbed to almost 80 million. And today, the drug problem is much more complex. Back in the 1960s, the problem was limited largely to heroin; now it includes coke, crack, methamphetamine (especially Ice), PCP (angel dust), and Ecstasy. Given the many problems that can accompany drugs, this means that the burden on society has increased as well.

THE USER'S VIEW

A large percentage of adolescents in the United States have, by the age of 18, used both legal and illegal drugs to get high. According to the 1996 *Monitoring the Future* study, put out by the National Institute on Drug Abuse, the overall use of illegal drugs among 8th, 10th, and 12th graders is up nationwide. Certainly, legal drugs have their dangers as well: tobacco increases one's risk of cancer, and alcohol can lead to fatal accidents. But illegal drugs bring about additional and, in many cases, more serious concerns. What should be of great concern to teenagers is the fact that most users of designer drugs die not from the chronic, long-term effects of their drugs of choice, but from one-time overdoses. Since

In many cases, addicts must turn to robbery or other criminal behaviors in order to support their drug habits.

the lethal effects of these drugs usually occur during a single episode of use, it's typically the young rather than the old who die from them.

Illegal drug users often argue that society has no right to restrict or even worry about their drug taking. "It's none of their business," they insist. "What I do with my life is my concern." Beyond the legal and moral issues surrounding such comments, the fact is that people do more than increase the likelihood of harming themselves when they take drugs. They can hurt others as well, regardless of whether they intended to. Designer drug users may believe they can handle their drug of choice, but given the unpredictability of these substances, users can't always know how they'll react. Certain drugs, like PCP, increase the odds of a user becoming violent, which means something or someone is likely to be harmed. One violent user may mean only one or two incidents. But thousands of such users add up to an increase in crimes against society.

SOCIETY'S VIEW

A study published in the December 1996 issue of the *Journal of the American Academy of Child and Adolescent Psychiatry* examined the progression from childhood aggression to adolescent drug use to delinquency over a 20-year period. The findings suggested that drug-use patterns can lead to criminal activity and violence, theft, vandalism, and aggression by reducing inhibitions in the teenager and young adult. Many teens in the population studied were found to commit crimes in order to obtain money to purchase drugs. A large percentage of these stole money, either from their parents or from strangers, to support their drug use. They also associated with, and often idolized, other drug users, some of whom were also delinquent. Another mediating link between drug use and delinquency was the adolescent's relations with family members. Drug use was seen to strain the parent-child relationship, which, in turn, caused the teen to turn away from conventional attitudes and turn toward later delinquent behavior.

In the long run, society also incurs the costs of rehabilitating drug users, which may include imprisonment, treatment, or both. If the user has children, they too need to be taken care of by others. Drug use can lead to substance abuse and dependence—a major public health problem in this country. In the general population, the number of persons addicted to or in trouble with various substances is enormous. Addictions to illegal drugs—including cocaine, heroin, LSD (lysergic acid diethylamide), PCP, and Ecstasy—are found in a total of more than three million users. Although these figures reflect adults and adolescents combined, those between the ages of 15 and 24 years show more cases of drug dependence than any other age group.

In the case of methamphetamine, the number of addicts admitted to emergency rooms across the country more than doubled from 2,400 in 1991 to 6,800 in 1996. Most of these incidents occurred in the western

DRUG DEALING IS NOT
A LUCRATIVE BUSINESS

Television shows and movies often portray drug dealers as rich and powerful, driving luxury automobiles and wearing lots of gold jewelry. But dealing drugs is not an easy way to get rich; in fact, a drug dealer looking for customers outside the local fast-food restaurant may make less than the person flipping burgers inside.

A study by economist Steven Levitt of the University of Chicago and sociologist Sudhir Venkatesh of Harvard University found that the bottom-level dealers make just $3 an hour. The only ones who make money on drugs are the gang leaders, who can make as much as $65 an hour while confining the risks—arrest, murder by a rival gang member—to the low-level pushers. And because of poverty in the inner cities, there are always youths attracted by the glamour of gangs and drugs who are willing to fill these dealer positions.

"There's the mythology that the media has built about the lucrativeness of pushing drugs, but the lessons of introductory economics suggest it can't be true," Levitt told Forbes magazine in August 1998. "These are kids with very low skills and there's a reserve army of them waiting to get into the gang. Competition would suggest that the employer [the gang leader] has all the power in this relationship."

Most youths join a gang in hopes of rising to the top of the power structure, and thus achieving the power and money that come with being leader of the gang. However, in the violent world of drug gangs, few ever reach that level. "Right now, the kids are completely getting the calculation wrong about what the likelihood is they're going to rise up in the gang," Venkatesh told Forbes. Educating gang members about the truth of the drug "business" may lead some of them to take legitimate jobs or inspire them to remain in school and get an education.

half of the United States, with San Diego, San Francisco, and Los Angeles among the leading cities in the nation for meth-related deaths, according to the White House Office of National Drug Control Policy's summer 1997 report, *Pulsecheck*. Again, the hospitalization of one person who has overdosed may not mean much to society as a whole, but the cumulative effect of thousands of users being treated for overdoses eventually feeds into higher health care costs for everyone.

There are many social problems that are related to drug use in the United States. Among these are homelessness, domestic violence, and the spread of AIDS.

In addition to the problem of increased crime and the significant health care costs associated with drug abuse, our society must deal with many other social problems resulting from drugs. Among the many social problems that illegal drug use contributes to are domestic violence, the spread of acquired immunodeficiency syndrome (AIDS) and other diseases, homelessness, education deficiencies, and increases in the number of welfare recipients.

Illegal drug use contributes to a weaker workforce, which translates into a less competitive economy. The trade in designer drugs—including underground laboratories, dealers, and users—has led in some cases to the downfall of local communities because of increased violent crime. On a smaller scale, individual neighborhoods in which the illegal labs operate can also be undermined. With labs being set up everywhere from rural areas and suburban neighborhoods to urban tenements, their toxic and explosive fumes pose a serious threat to the health and safety of many communities across the country.

Educating young adults about the negative effects of drugs is necessary to reduce the number of users in the United States.

6

CURRENT TREATMENT OPTIONS

Drug use among teens has many different levels of severity. Some may just be experimenting or using the illegal substances occasionally; others may be chronic users who have developed a severe dependence on the drug. The likelihood that some adolescents will go from simply trying drugs to developing substance dependence has a lot to do with their individual personality, genetic makeup, family situation, and psychiatric problems. Though drug addiction is never inevitable—some users of designer drugs never become addicted—the more a person uses the drugs, the higher the risk.

Most teenagers use designer drugs only occasionally, but excessive use can lead to severe disruption in adolescent development. The earlier that chronic users are identified, the better. Experimentation with drugs typically starts around 12 or 13 years old, so parents and teachers of junior high school students are usually the adults best placed to detect drug use. In very young teenagers, involvement, concern, and control by parents have a strong influence on behavior. According to the Partnership for a Drug-Free America, drug use is significantly lower among children who learn about the risks of drugs at home. Yet, only 28 percent of teens—just over one in four—say they've learned a great deal about the dangers of drugs from their parents.

The severity of a drug problem—from use to dependence to abuse—is often determined by the age of the individual when he or she first starts using drugs. The earlier the onset, the higher the probability that the individual will use drugs frequently or even abuse drugs as an adult. For teens who choose to experiment with drugs, intervention by parents, siblings, friends, and others may be all it takes to stop them from continuing toward abuse or dependence. The ones who do start abusing drugs may require treatment to help them quit.

A group of former substance abusers discuss their problems in a group therapy session. Group therapy is useful in reducing the sense of isolation that may lead some people to use drugs.

Most people don't go voluntarily into treatment, because more often than not, they believe that they're not the ones with the problem. Rather, they may feel that everyone around them just doesn't understand them. It often takes time—usually not until they stop using the drug and notice improvement—to admit and want to overcome their problems. In the case of teens, they may be forced into treatment by their parents, or by a judge who gives them a choice: jail or rehabilitation.

TYPES OF TREATMENT PROGRAMS

Until the mid-1960s, most doctors believed that drug addiction was incurable. Many felt that abusers could be helped to overcome their physical cravings for the drug through brief periods of detoxification, usually with a treatment program to help a person remove drugs from the body. However, although the drugs were withdrawn from the body, the addict's psychological dependency remained, because doctors had not yet developed ways to treat this aspect of addiction.

In those years, drug addicts were likely to be admitted to psychiatric hospitals for extended stays. Today, such treatment is extremely rare, considered a last resort for the most severe cases. Instead of treating users as patients, who are just passive recipients of treatment, most programs today are based on self-help, in which an individual takes an active part in his or her recovery. Currently, the most common kinds of treatment programs include outpatient clinics and treatment, and residential short-term inpatient programs, each of which is explained in this chapter.

The first step in any modern treatment program is for the participant to recognize that drug use interferes significantly with all aspects of his or her life. To eliminate this interference, the person has to understand that all drug use must cease. From that point, each addict must be evaluated to determine the particular program that will be most effective for him or her. Individual therapy may uncover issues of poor self-esteem, depression, severe family problems, and/or preexisting psychological disorders. To address these issues fully and to provide the user with support, family or group therapy may be necessary. Parental counseling also may be very effective in resolving disturbed family interaction and disciplinary issues. Many people show significant denial and sometimes open hostility in the early stages of therapy, so counselors and therapists have to convince them that changing their behavior can only improve their lives.

OUTPATIENT TREATMENT

Outpatient programs generally provide a range of services from day-long programs to group or individual sessions on a weekly basis. These are called outpatient because the participants are not hospitalized or confined to a treatment facility, although they visit a hospital or

As part of therapy for drug abuse, it is helpful to speak with a psychiatrist one-on-one. Therapy can help improve a teen's self-esteem and teach how to make lifestyle changes to avoid using drugs.

clinic for their treatment. Patients may be involved in such programs for weeks, months, or longer if necessary. In many cases, treatment will involve a combination of services like individual therapy, family analysis, and group sessions. Counselors help patients with vocational skills and educational activities. Depending on the drug from which the patient is recovering, medication may be prescribed. For example, someone who has become addicted to meperidine might receive gradually decreasing doses of methadone, a drug that is typically used to treat opioid addition because it eases withdrawal symptoms. On the whole, however, most programs emphasize drug-free treatment.

Outpatient treatment is also often anchored by a 12-step program similar to that of Alcoholics Anonymous. Initially, contact with the program should be a major focus of the person's life. But as each person progresses, the degree of involvement is reduced and the program becomes more peripheral to his or her daily activities.

Psychiatric therapy may be a crucial treatment option for patients who have drug abuse problems, with the primary goal being abstinence from drugs. In addition to improving self-awareness, therapy can help teenage drug users to make certain lifestyle changes, such as avoiding those persons, places, and things related to drug use. Those peers the patient associates with getting high tend to be too closely, sometimes exclusively, linked to drug use and may have little to offer someone who has stopped using. Such changes may also require attending intervention groups, changing schools, or using a chemical dependency or therapeutic community program.

A patient may also have an accompanying psychological disorder that may have led to or was uncovered by the use of drugs. Once the person is drug-free, individual therapy can help him or her resolve particular underlying conflicts. Addressing such issues in therapy also serves as an effective tool to help the reformed drug abuser prevent possible relapses.

Teens with problems relating to drug use typically still live with their parents and siblings; hence, their behavior has a significant impact on family relations. Family therapy may be critical to helping the family learn how to support and encourage the teen at home. Ideally, the family and the therapist can also function together as a source of support throughout the stages of treatment. These stages often focus on improving family communication patterns, altering parental expectations, and addressing parental or sibling drug use. Ultimately, therapists may encourage the family to draw continued, posttherapy support from a carefully selected group of family and friends.

Group therapy has become the most frequently used treatment for all types of drug abuse. Usually consisting of 10 to 15 teens and a counselor, drug treatment groups give teens the opportunity to deal with their particular issues, aided by group members. Ideally, the group will help them identify suppressed feelings, see how addiction has hurt themselves and others, and begin to see the need for change. By sharing their feelings and listening to what other group members tell them about themselves, teens are encouraged to discover who they are. Education in regard to the causes and effects of drug use is often included. Groups are useful in teaching socialization and problem-solving skills and may reduce the sense of isolation that people who abuse drugs often feel.

Treatment procedures modeled after the Alcoholics Anonymous 12-step programs have proven useful for many who abuse drugs. Members of these groups accept dependence on a "higher power" and are encouraged to adhere to steps, traditions, and value systems based primarily on sobriety. In the past, teens who are primarily dependent on designer drugs have not participated extensively in these groups. Recently, however, many meetings of Drugs Anonymous and other self-help groups have become more sensitive to their needs. Whereas 12-step programs encourage adults to continue to think of themselves as recovering addicts, they treat teens somewhat differently. Teen drug programs may concentrate on showing members healthier age-related behavior and teaching them better communication skills. After a year or more of abstinence and appropriate social adjustment, young individuals are encouraged to think of themselves as similar to their peers, though with the recognition that they continue to be at increased risk of drug abuse.

SHORT-TERM INPATIENT TREATMENT

Once primarily for alcohol abuse treatment, short-term inpatient treatment programs expanded into drug abuse treatment in the 1980s. Rarely would someone who uses designer drugs be hospitalized, but it has happened. Occasionally with severe abuse or behavioral problems, especially among teenagers, inpatient intervention may be necessary.

Before an individual is admitted to a hospital or clinic, he or she must meet one or more of the following criteria:

- The inability to cease drug use despite the help of outpatient treatment
- The presence of psychological (or, in rare cases, medical) conditions that require close observation and treatment, such as severe depressive symptoms, psychotic states, or extreme debilitation
- The absence of adequate psychological and social support groups that might help the person to stop taking drugs
- The necessity to interrupt a living situation that reinforces continued drug taking
- The need to enhance motivation or break through denial.

Support from family and friends is an important component of treatment for drug abuse or addiction.

Short-term inpatient programs typically keep patients for up to a month. Most of these programs focus on medical stabilization, abstinence from drugs, and lifestyle changes. Staff members are primarily medical professionals and trained counselors. For teens, the disadvantage of inpatient treatment is that it disrupts their lives and school careers, reinforces their insecurity about their abilities or even their sanity, and often stigmatizes them.

RESIDENTIAL TREATMENT

Residential treatment is basically a transitional living situation for teenagers who are not yet ready to return home from inpatient treatment. These adolescents may need such a setting either because they didn't make enough progress as an inpatient or because they have an unresolved family issue at home, such as a parent who abuses drugs. Residential treatment is typically referred to as secondary or extended treatment, and is set up in two forms: halfway houses and therapeutic communities.

Halfway houses provide a supportive, drug-free living environment. A person's stay typically lasts from two to six months. The household may have 10 to 20 adolescents who live together in a supervised setting and share responsibility for maintaining the house. They do the grocery shopping, cook meals, do housework, and wash their own clothes. Teenagers still attend school during the day and they are encouraged to hold a part-time job. Treatment is kept at a minimum, typically consisting of support group meetings.

Originally developed to treat heroin addicts, therapeutic communities today focus on multidrug users and adolescents. They focus not only on helping users to become drug free, but also on understanding and overcoming the underlying causes of their drug abuse. The communities place an emphasis on patient socialization and offer programs that run from three months to two years. Some communities require residents to be separated from the outside world; others do not.

A supervised group of adolescents live in dormitories and learn to work for the betterment of the entire group. They do chores, cook meals, and generally maintain the facility. As they progress in treatment and perform well at their jobs, members may be promoted to more responsible positions—a reward that bolsters self-confidence and enhances self-esteem. Varying levels of treatment are found among communities, but group therapy sessions are usually strongly confrontational. Most programs offer counseling, seminars, group and family therapy, education, and vocational counseling. Many therapeutic communities also have wilderness programs, in which teens can go camping, canoeing, and white-water rafting. In addition to building self-confidence, these experiences show adolescents that it's possible to have fun without using drugs.

APPENDIX

A SELF-TEST FOR TEENAGERS

How Are Alcohol and Drugs Affecting Your Life?

---

1. Do you use alcohol or other drugs to build self-confidence? ❑ YES ❑ NO

2. Do you ever drink or get high immediately after you have a problem at home or at school? ❑ YES ❑ NO

3. Have you ever missed school due to use of alcohol or other drugs? ❑ YES ❑ NO

4. Does it bother you if someone says that you use too much alcohol or other drugs? ❑ YES ❑ NO

5. Have you started hanging out with a heavy drinking or drug-using crowd? ❑ YES ❑ NO

6. Is the use of alcohol or other drugs affecting your reputation? ❑ YES ❑ NO

7. Do you feel guilty or bummed out after using alcohol or other drugs? ❑ YES ❑ NO

8. Do you feel more at ease on a date when drinking or using other drugs? ❑ YES ❑ NO

9. Have you gotten into trouble at home for using alcohol or other drugs? ❑ YES ❑ NO

10. Do you borrow money or "do without" other things to buy alcohol and other drugs? ❑ YES ❑ NO

11. Do you feel a sense of power when you use alcohol or other drugs? ❑ YES ❑ NO

12. Have you lost friends since you started using alcohol or other drugs? ❏ YES ❏ NO

13. Do your friends use less alcohol or other drugs than you do? ❏ YES ❏ NO

14. Do you drink or use other drugs until your supply is all gone? ❏ YES ❏ NO

15. Do you ever wake up and wonder what happened the night before? ❏ YES ❏ NO

16. Have you ever been busted or hospitalized due to alcohol or use of illicit drugs? ❏ YES ❏ NO

17. Do you "turn off" any studies or lectures about alcohol or illicit drug use? ❏ YES ❏ NO

18. Do you think you have a problem with alcohol or other drugs? ❏ YES ❏ NO

19. Has there ever been someone in your family with a drinking or other drug problem? ❏ YES ❏ NO

20. Could you have a problem with alcohol or other drugs? ❏ YES ❏ NO

Purchase or public possession of alcohol is illegal for anyone under the age of 21 everywhere in the United States. Aside from the fact that you may be breaking the law by using alcohol and/or illicit drugs, if you answer "yes" to any three of the above questions, you may be at risk for developing alcoholism and/or dependence on another drug. If you answer "yes" to five of these questions, you should seek professional help immediately. Call (800) NCA-CALL or one of the other toll-free numbers listed in Appendix B for a referral to someone who can help you.

Source: National Council on Alcoholism and Drug Dependence (NCADD)
12 West 21st Street, New York, NY 10010

APPENDIX

ORGANIZATIONS AND RESOURCE CENTERS

Many national organizations providing families with education, support, and counseling services are listed below. Many also have local chapters. For additional information or treatment option, look in the yellow pages of your telephone book under "drug abuse" and "counseling."

Addiction Research Foundation (ARF)
33 Russell Street
Toronto, Ontario M5S 2S1

Alcohol and Drug Dependency Information and Counseling Services
2471 1/2 Portage Avenue, #2
Winnipeg, MB R3J 0N6
(204) 831-1999

American Counsel for Drug Education
204 Monroe Street, Suite 110
Rockville, MD 20850
(301) 294-0600
(800) DRUG-HELP
www.acde.org

Families in Action
National Drug Abuse Center
3845 North Druid Hills Road, Suite 300
Decatur, GA 30033
(404) 325-5799

Friday Night Live
California Department of Alcohol
  and Drug Programs
11 Capitol Mall, Room 223
Sacramento, CA 95814
(916) 445-7456

Hazelden Educational Materials
Pleasant Valley Road
PO Box 176
Center City, MN 55012-0176
(800) 328-9000

Nar-Anon Family Groups
PO Box 2562
Palos Verdes Peninsula, CA 90274
(310) 547-5800

Narcotics Anonymous
PO Box 9999
Van Nuys, CA 94109
(818) 773-9999
www.wsoinc.com

Narcotics Anonymous
PO Box 7500, Station A
Toronto, ON M5W 1P9
(416) 691-9519

National Clearinghouse for Alcohol and Drug Information (NCADI)
PO Box 2345
Rockville, MD 20847-2345
(800) 729-6686
www.health.org

National Council on Alcoholism and Drug Dependence (NCADD)
12 West 21st Street
New York, NY 10010
(800) 622-2255
(212) 206-6770
www.ncadd.org

National Families in Action
2296 Henderson Mill Road, Suite 204
Atlanta, GA 30345
(404) 934-6364

National Federation of Parents for Drug-Free Youth
9551 Big Bend
St. Louis, MO 63122
(314) 968-1322

National Institute on Drug Abuse (NIDA)
11400 Rockville Pike
Rockville, MD 20852
(301) 443-1124
hotline (800) 662-HELP

National Prevention Network
444 North Capitol Street NW, Suite 642
Washington, DC 20001
(202) 783-6868

Parents Educational Resource Center
1660 South Amphlett Blvd., Suite 200
San Mateo, CA 94402-2508
(415) 655-2410

Parents Resource Institute for Drug Education, Inc. (PRIDE)
Hurt Building
50 Hurt Plaza, Suite 210
Atlanta, GA 30303
(404) 651-2548
(800) 241-7941

Phoenix House
164 W 74th Street
New York, NY 10023
(800) DRUG-HELP
(212) 595-5810 ext. 7510
www.phoenixhouse.org,
www.drughelp.org

Phoenix House
11600 Eldridge Avenue
Lake View Terrace, CA 91342
(800) DRUG-HELP
(818) 896-1121 ext. 4053
www.phoenixhouse.org,
www.drughelp.org

Tough Love hotline
(800) 333-1069

APPENDIX

INTERNET RESOURCES

www.drug-abuse.com/information/treatment

www.drughelp.org/research/methamphetamine.htm

www.emory.edu./NFIA/DRUG_INFO

www.fadaa.org/resource/jtf/designerdrugs.html

www.nida.nih.gov/NIDACapsules/NCPCP.html. NIDA Capsule Series, C-86-08. Revised September, 1997.

www.nida.nih.gov/ResearchReports/

www.phoenixhouse.org/treatment/

www.ravesafe.org.za/e-research_1997.htm. Reproduced from The Independent, London, October 1997.

www.tcada.state.tx.us/research/

www.well.com/user/woa/fshallu.htm

APPENDIX

BIBLIOGRAPHY

Alvergue, A. *Ecstasy: The Danger of False Euphoria.* New York: The Rosen Publishing Group, 1998.

Baberg, H. T., et al. "Amphetamine Use: Return of an Old Scourge in a Consultation Psychiatry Setting." *American Journal of Psychiatry* 153, no 6 (June 1996).

Bordwine Beeder, A. and R. B. Millman. "Cannabis Abuse and Dependence." *Treatments of Psychiatric Disorders,* 2d ed., sec 4. Washington D.C.: American Psychiatric Press, 1995.

Brook, J. S., M. Whiteman, S. J. Finch, And P. Cohen. "Young Adult Drug Use and Delinquency: Childhood Antecedents and Adolescent Mediators." *Journal of the American Academy of Child and Adolescent Psychiatry* (December 1996).

Cattarello, A. M., R. R. Clayton, and C. G. Leukefeld. "Adolescent Alcohol and Drug Abuse." *Review of Psychiatry* 14, sec 1. Washington D.C.: American Psychiatric Press, 1995.

Dana Alliance for Brain Initiatives. "Delivering Results: A Program Report on Brain Research, New York, 1996 ." NIDA Notes, March/April 1997 (http://165.112.78.61/NIDA_Notes/NNVol12N2/Ecstasy.html).

Drugs, Society, and Behavior (1993/94 annual editions). Ed. by E. Goode. State University of New York at Stony Brook, The Dushkin Publishing Group, Inc.

Dupre, D., N. Miller, M. Gold, and K. Rospenda. "Initiation and Progression of Alcohol, Marijuana, and Cocaine Use Among Adolescent Abusers." *American Journal on Addictions* 4, no 1 (January 1995).

Duryea, B. "3 Clubgoers Overdose on Illegal Drug GHB." *St. Petersburg Times,* October 2, 1996.

Falkowski, C. "Drug Abuse Trends in the Minneapolis-St. Paul Metropolitan Area (press release)." Hazelden Institute and the Butler Center for Research and Learning, June 16, 1998.

Frances, R. J. and J. E. Franklin Jr. "Alcohol and Other Psychoactive Substance Use Disorders." *APP Textbook of Psychiatry*, 2d ed., sec 3. Washington D.C.: American Psychiatric Press, 1994.

Greenblatt, J. C: "Gamma Hydroxy Butyrate (GHB) Abuse In the United States." A Working Paper by Office of Applied Studies (OAS), Substance Abuse and Mental Health Services Administration. Rockville, MD: September, 1997 (www.health.org).

Kandel, D. B. and M. Davies. "High School Students Who Use Crack and Other Drugs." *Archives of General Psychiatry* 53 (1996).

Kirsch, M. M. *Designer Drugs.* CompCare Publications, 1986.

Kleber, H. "Substance Abuse." *Review of Psychiatry* 14, sec 1. Washington D.C.: American Psychiatric Press, 1995.

Kleber, H. and M. Galanter. "Substance-Related Disorders: Introduction." *Treatments of Psychiatric Disorders*, 2d ed., sec 4. Washington D.C.: American Psychiatric Press, 1995.

Kleber, H. D., et al. "Pharmacological Treatments for Narcotic and Opioid Addictions." *Treatments of Psychiatric Disorders*, 2d ed., sec 4. Washington D.C.: American Psychiatric Press, 1995.

Kuhn, C., et al. *Buzzed: The Straight Facts About the Most Used and Abused Drugs From Alcohol to Ecstasy.* New York: W. W. Norton & Co., 1998.

Massing, M. "The Fix: Under the Nixon Administration, America Had an Effective Drug Policy. We Should Restore It (Nixon Was Right)." New York: Simon & Schuster, 1998.

Merikan, J. R. "Review of *Marabou Stork Nightmares* (a novel by Irvine Welsh)." *American Journal of Psychiatry* 153, no 12 (December 1996).

"Methamphetamine Trends in Five Western States and Hawaii." Special Report by White House Office of National Drug Control Policy, summer 1997 (www.drugfreeamerica.org/meth: PULSE CHECK).

Milhorn Jr., H. T. *Drug and Alcohol Abuse: The Authoritative Guide for Parents, Teachers, and Counselors.* New York: Plenum Press, 1994.

"Monitoring the Future Study." University of Michigan, 1997 (www.drugfreeamerica.org/meth: NIDA).

Turney, L. "Designer Drugs: Deadly by Design." D.I.N. Publications, April 1998 (http://doitnow.org/pages/159.html).

Walter, H. J. "Substance Abuse and Substance Use Disorders." *Treatments of Psychiatric Disorders*, 2d ed., sec 2. Washington D.C.: American Psychiatric Press, 1995.

APPENDIX

FURTHER READING

Alvergue, A. *Ecstasy: The Danger of False Euphoria*. New York: Rosen Publishing Group, 1998.

American Psychiatric Association. *Diagnostic and Statistical Manual of Mental Disorders*, 4th ed. Washington, D.C.: American Psychiatric Press, 1994.

———. *Treatment of Psychiatric Disorders*, 2d ed. 2 vols. Washington, D.C.: American Psychiatric Press, 1994.

Carroll, Marilyn. *PCP: The Dangerous Angel*. New York: Chelsea House Publishers, 1992.

Cohen, Richard S. *The Love Drug : Marching to the Beat of Ecstasy*. Binghamton, N.Y.: The Haworth Press, 1998.

Croft, Jennifer. *PCP: High Risk on the Streets*. New York: Rosen Publishing Group, 1998.

Garman, J. Frederick. *Methamphetamine & "Ice."* New York: William Gladden Foundation, 1992.

Kirsch, M. M. *Designer Drugs*. New York: CompCare Publications, 1986.

Kuhn, C., et al. *Buzzed: The Straight Facts About the Most Used and Abused Drugs From Alcohol to Ecstasy*. New York: W. W. Norton & Co., 1998.

Lawrence, Clayton. *Designer Drugs*. New York: Rosen Publishing Group, 1997.

Milhorn Jr., H. T. *Drug and Alcohol Abuse: The Authoritative Guide for Parents, Teachers, and Counselors*. New York: Plenum Press, 1994.

Moser, Leslie E. *Crack, Cocaine, Methamphetamine and Ice*. New York: Multi Media Productions, 1990.

Newman, Gerald, and Eleanor Newman Layfield. *PCP*. Springfield, N.J.: Enslow Publishers, 1997.

Perkins, Scott W. *Drug Identification: Designer and Club Drugs Quick Reference Guide.* New York: Alliance Press, 1998.

Redda, Kinfe, and Charles A. Walker. *Cocaine, Marijuana, Designer Drugs : Chemistry, Pharmacology, and Behavior.* Boca Raton, Fla.: CRC Press, 1989.

Robbins, Paul R. *Designer Drugs.* Springfield, N.J.: Enslow Publishers, 1995.

APPENDIX

GLOSSARY

Amphetamine: A chemical compound that acts as a stimulant to the central nervous system, causes an increase in brain activity, and contributes to increased energy levels, sleeplessness, and a general sense of well-being in the user. Amphetamines include speed and methamphetamines, and cause dangerous side effects.

Aphrodisiac: A substance that arouses sexual desire. When taken in small doses, the designer drugs Ecstasy and GHB (Gamma-hydroxybutyric Acid) are considered chemical aphrodisiacs.

Contaminant: An element added to a pure substance that makes it impure or dangerous. Many people who manufacture designer drugs have been known to add contaminants such as laxatives, antihistamines, other drugs, and even strychnine (rat poison) to increase the drug's weight and consequently, its street price. However, this also increases the risk of dangerous, and unexpected, side effects.

Derivative: A chemical substance that can be made from another chemical substance in one or more steps. Derivatives of the drug opium include heroin and morphine; these are called opiates.

Designer drugs: Illegal chemical compounds designed, modified, and manufactured to have the same effects as the natural-source drugs they mimic. In many cases, however, the reactions to designer drugs are even stronger and more addictive than those of their natural counterparts. Ecstasy, PCP, crystal meth, and GHB are among the most popular designer drugs.

Ecstasy: A derivation of methamphetamine and amphetamine, Ecstasy is the most commonly used designer drug. It is often found at music-filled, all-night dance parties called raves, where its hallucinogenic side effects make it a popular choice among drug users.

Endorphins: Protein compounds released by the pituitary gland that act as natural painkillers and cause a feeling of euphoria, or intense well-being.

Endorphins are released when the body is in pain, or after prolonged exercise. They attach to the same receptors in the brain as chemicals like morphine and heroin.

Fentanyl: Originally produced as a nonaddictive replacement for heroin, this opioid is actually highly addictive and can be 100 times more powerful than heroin, depending on how it is manufactured. Like other opiates, fentanyl produces feelings of intense pleasure and well-being, followed by a calm drowsiness. China White is one of the most popular forms of fentanyl.

Flashbacks: Unpredictable, spontaneous memories of a previous drug-induced "trip" or fantasy that usually last a few minutes and may occur weeks, months, even years after the encounter, and without the user's having taken the drug again. Users of hallucinogens, such as Ecstasy and PCP, are especially likely to suffer these typically visual images, which range from formless colors to frightening hallucinations.

Gamma-hydroxybutyric Acid (GHB): A depressant and painkiller, GHB has gained notoriety in recent years as a "date rape drug," because people who take it may become open to assault. It is popular at night clubs and among partygoers.

Hallucinogen: A chemical substance that induces hallucinations, or imaginary perceptions. Hallucinogenic drugs have been shown to contribute to flashbacks, paranoia, and even psychosis.

Meperidine (MPPP): Also known by its trade name, Demerol, meperidine is an addictive drug that produces a euphoria similar to that of heroin; but because it is difficult to manufacture, careless or inexperienced chemists may inadvertently create poisonous by-products. One of these by-products, an impurity called MPTP, can cause irreversible brain damage with physical effects resembling severe symptoms of Parkinson's disease.

Methamphetamine: A stimulant that can be smoked, snorted, injected, or taken orally, methamphetamines are highly addictive and its users are subject to "bingeing" on the drug and then "crashing," or coming down quickly from a high. One of its most popular forms, crystal meth, has been dubbed the "cocaine of the '90s."

Opiate/opioid: Generic terms for all drugs derived from the opium poppy, or synthesized to have similar effects. Opiates are specifically those derived from the plant, while opioids include both natural and synthetic forms of the drug.

Phencyclidine (PCP): First introduced as a street drug in the late 1960s, PCP is known for its widely differing, and dangerous, side effects.

Psychosis: a mental derangement that can be caused by drug use and is characterized by loss of contact with reality.

Stimulant: a drug that produces a temporary increase of functional activity of an organism or any of its parts.

Synthesize: the production of a substance by the union of chemical elements, groups, or similar compounds, or the breaking down of a chemical compound. Designer drugs are synthesized, that is manufactured by a person, rather than found in nature.

Toxins: poisonous substances that are specific products of the metabolic activities of a living organism that can become toxic when introduced into human tissue. The toxins in a drug may cause permanent brain damage or death.

Withdrawal: the physical and mental symptoms that occur when a person who is physically dependent on a drug stops taking the drug. Withdrawal symptoms include physical distress similar to a bad case of the flu, including muscle aches and cramps, fever, vomiting, and weakness, as well as mental symptoms such as depression and hallucinations.

APPENDIX

PICTURE CREDITS

Senior Consulting Editor Carol C. Nadelson, M.D., is president and chief executive officer of the American Psychiatric Press, Inc., staff physician at Cambridge Hospital, and Clinical Professor of Psychiatry at Harvard Medical School. In addition to her work with the American Psychiatric Association, which she served as vice president in 1981–83 and president in 1985–86, Dr. Nadelson has been actively involved in other major psychiatric organizations, including the Group for the Advancement of Psychiatry, the American College of Psychiatrists, the Association for Academic Psychiatry, the American Association of Directors of Psychiatric Residency Training Programs, the American Psychosomatic Society, and the American College of Mental Health Administrators. In addition, she has been a consultant to the Psychiatric Education Branch of the National Institute of Mental Health and has served on the editorial boards of several journals. Doctor Nadelson has received many awards, including the Gold Medal Award for significant and ongoing contributions in the field of psychiatry, the Elizabeth Blackwell Award for contributions to the causes of women in medicine, and the Distinguished Service Award from the American College of Psychiatrists for outstanding achievements and leadership in the field of psychiatry.

Consulting Editor Claire E. Reinburg, M.A., is editorial director of the American Psychiatric Press, Inc., which publishes about 60 new books and six journals a year. She is a graduate of Georgetown University in Washington, D.C., where she earned bachelor of arts and master of arts degrees in English. She is a member of the Council of Biology Editors, the Women's National Book Association, the Society for Scholarly Publishing, and Washington Book Publishers.

As director of Write Stuff Editorial Service in New York City, **Elizabeth Russell Connelly** has written and edited for medical and business journals, trade magazines, high-tech firms, and various book publishers. She earned an MBA from New York University's Stern School in 1993 and a certificate in language studies from Freiburg Universitaet (Switzerland) in 1985. Her published work includes a global studies book for young adults; more than 14 Access travel guides covering North America, the Caribbean, and Europe; and several volumes in Chelsea House Publishers' ENCYCLOPEDIA OF PSYCHOLOGICAL DISORDERS, including *A World Upside Down and Backwards: Reading and Learning Disorders, Through a Glass Darkly: The Psychological Effects of Marijuana and Hashish,* and *Child Abuse and Neglect: Examining the Psychological Components.*